households
and holiness

households
and holiness

The Religious Culture
of Israelite Women

CAROL MEYERS

FORTRESS PRESS
MINNEAPOLIS

HOUSEHOLDS AND HOLINESS
The Religious Culture of Israelite Women

Cover design: Laurie Ingram
Cover image: Figurines of Asherah, Canaanite,
999–600 BC Photo © Zev Radovan / Bridgeman Images

Print ISBN: 978-1-5064-8860-8
eBook ISBN: 978-1-5064-8861-5

Contents

Preface

Several years ago, the organizers of the XVII Congress of the International Organization for the Study of the Old Testament invited me to give a keynote lecture in the unit on the topic "Theology of the Old Testament, History of Israel's Religion." They requested that I consider the impact of sociological and/or gender studies on the study of Israel's religion. I wrote a paper that I hoped would do both and delivered it at the Congress meeting in Basel in 2001. Titled "From Household to House of Yahweh—Women's Religious Culture in Ancient Israel," the paper subsequently appeared in the Vetus Testamentum Supplement in which all the conference papers were published.[1]

I am grateful to the publishers for permission for it to appear in this series. I am also pleased that the editors of Fortress Press, in particular K. C. Hanson, suggested that the paper, which features a topic—women's religious lives in biblical antiquity—that would have a wider audience than the readership of Vetus Testamentum Supplements, might appear in a somewhat revised and expanded form in this edition.

CHAPTER ONE

Introduction

In the late nineteenth century, an Englishwoman named Lucy M. J. Garnett traveled throughout the Ottoman Empire for a decade, observing the behaviors of the women "of the East," as she called them: women in Christian, Jewish, and Muslim communities. She published her investigations, which were informed by the meager existing ethnological and ethnographic literature of her day, in two volumes (1890 and 1891).[1] The information in her books had the effect of making those women of the East visible. Without the data she provided, as another traveler noted, "the female sex may be said not to have existed at all."[2]

The situation is not quite so dire when it comes to investigating another group of women of the

East, ancient Israelite women. Already at the turn of the nineteenth century, not long after Lucy Garnett's work appeared, biblical scholars—all of them men—entered into a lively debate about the role of women in biblical religion.[3] Some actually asserted that women's participation was broader and more significant than commonly supposed. One scholar, for example, mounted extensive and careful arguments against the then current view that women were disqualified from cultic activity. He concluded,

> The Semites in general, and the Hebrews in particular, and the latter especially in the earlier periods of their history, exhibit no tendency to discriminate between man and woman so far as regards participation in religious practices, but that woman participated in all the essentials of the cult, both as worshipper and official.[4]

Moreover, pioneer feminists involved in the suffrage movement sponsored their own projects of biblical interpretation. Eager to combat the use of the Bible to deny women civil rights, they embarked upon major projects—most notably Elizabeth Cady Stanton's *The Woman's Bible*[5]—employing a feminist hermeneutic. But the religious establishment in Europe and the United States for the most part took the opposite view. Julius Wellhausen, perhaps the most prominent and influential biblical scholar of modern times, claimed, at the end of the nineteenth century, that women had no political rights and therefore no place in religion.[6] And he was not alone in such assertions.

Whether viewed positively or negatively, at least Israelite women were partially in view. As the twentieth century wore on, however, interest in their lives and roles faded. For example, women are virtually nonexistent in the mid-century work of Georg Fohrer, *History of Israelite Religion*.[7] The same can be said for Yehezkel Kaufmann's multivolume *History of Israelite Religion from the Beginning to the End of the Second Temple*.[8] Women had become as unseen in biblical studies as in the towns of the Ottoman Empire. But this invisibility was not to last.

By the closing decades of the twentieth century, the growing feminist movement in the Americas and on the Continent created a resurgence of attention to women in the biblical world.[9] This more recent scholarship has revisited, reconsidered, revised, and revamped existing notions of the religion of Israelite women. A wide variety of approaches and methodologies are represented in this new scholarship.[10] Some studies, eager to claim biblical authority for women's present-day aspirations, are highly positive if not apologetic. At the other end of the spectrum are decidedly critical assessments; they are indignant at what is perceived as male domination and female subordination and thus assert that the Bible represents irredeemably misogynist views. These opposing perspectives have evoked vigorous debate and have influenced biblical scholarship. That is, studies of Israelite religion no longer ignore women; and meetings of biblical study associations, notably the venerable Society of Biblical Literature, devote significant numbers of sessions and plenaries to the topic of women and the Bible. Whether supportive of or finding fault with the place of women in the Bible and the biblical world, however, none of the discussions succeed, in my view, in truly understanding the part that religion played in the lives of Israelite women and, just as important, the role that women played in the religious lives of all Israelites. I can suggest several reasons for this.

For one thing, feminist biblical study, whether conducted by women or by men, still tends to represent masculinized approaches.[11] For two thousand years, the description and interpretation of religious experience in general and of scripture in particular have been carried out almost exclusively by male religious professionals—clergy as well as scholars.[12] Because men were the interpreters of scripture, their experience was held as the norm. Feminist biblical scholarship has not sufficiently broken away from

Western male models of what constitutes religion. Consequently, it often views women's experiences and practices, wherever visible in the Hebrew Bible, as marginal—as not "real religion."[13] The religious lives of Israelite women are seen as circumscribed by male religious culture. Perhaps this has happened, in part, because the study of religion in modern academic circles, especially ones dominated by Protestant interpretive traditions, tends to equate religion with theology. In this conceptualization, Israelite religion is first and foremost the belief in or worship of Yahweh (or some other deity or deities).[14] Belief systems are seen as primary, with praxis as secondary or derivative. Exploring the nature of the deity with respect to gender and belief thus becomes privileged over investigating the religious behaviors of women.

Because of this tendency to focus on belief rather than practice, attention to women often centers on whether they worshiped a particular goddess, such as Asherah, rather than on what their religious concerns were and what steps they took to deal with those concerns. Focusing on female deities as a possible path toward understanding women's religion is triply flawed:

1. It assumes that goddesses are linked mainly to female worshipers, when in fact people of both

genders apparently participated in cultic practices directed toward deities of either gender. For example, the exchange between Jeremiah and the group of people who had fled to Egypt (Jeremiah 44) suggests that the goddess cult implicated in that confrontation involved participation of both genders, even if their specific cultic acts may have differed.[15] And, of course, that women worshiped male deities is apparent throughout the Bible. Women are among the worshipers of Yahweh, who is referred to in the Bible with masculine language and is represented primarily with andromorphic (male) imagery, although occasional gynomorphic (female) images appear.[16]

2. It objectifies the female by looking at female symbols—the goddesses—as objects of veneration.[17]

3. It gives too little consideration to religion as *activity* in women's lives.

Another problem is that feminist biblical study has not been successful enough in separating itself from the perspective of the biblical authors. This too has three shortcomings:

1. Most of the producers of scripture were elite, urban males such as priests and members of the

royal bureaucracy, probably addressing other men; and even the prophets, perhaps not urban or elite, were mainly men.[18] Their goals and interests rarely included the concerns or practices of women.

2. The perspective of the producers of scripture was for the most part national and communal, not familial and domestic. Biblical texts lead us to ask questions about whether women were allowed in the temple precincts or whether they could offer sacrifices at community festivals, not about what religious acts women may have performed in their own households, every day.

3. Some laws, narratives, and prophetic diatribes condemn what women (as well as men) do; taken out of context they provide a distorted, negative view of practices that may have played a very positive role in women's lives.

This last point refers to texts that set forth what was deemed to be acceptable and proper in cultic practice and who were acceptable and proper cultic practitioners. Biblical texts seem to limit religious leadership to men in their specification of a male-only priesthood. These texts are understood to mean that women were always excluded from such roles or that the few instances in which women appear as ritual professionals represent aberrant behavior. Women (as well as men) who practiced divination or necromancy, for example, are condemned in Lev 20:27, even though such cultic functionaries may have performed important services in helping people feel they could communicate with divine powers or deceased ancestors.[19]

Yet scholars have tended to see the women who performed these rituals as departing from or opposing accepted beliefs or established doctrine, even of inclining toward heresy. In other words, they have been inclined to accept those texts as having been normative for most Israelites for most of the biblical period, although we now realize that those texts and the viewpoints they represent may not have been widely accepted until relatively late in the biblical period, during the exile and in the postexilic period. Even Phyllis Bird, whose work in mining the Hebrew Bible for clues about women's religion is exemplary, looks at cultic practices mentioned in the Hebrew Bible as either "officially sanctioned" or "heterodox, sectarian."[20] Consider also Patrick Miller's recent study of *The Religion of Ancient Israel*, which does give some attention to women. However, because his whole approach is dominated by an orthodox (i.e., Yahwism) and heterodox/syncretistic binary, his attribution of a "significant role" for women in some aspects of Israelite religious life links them to its "heterodox aspects."[21] Such approaches inevitably privilege the religious activities of men over those of women.

Despite these conceptual problems, late-twentieth-century scholarship succeeded in establishing that women were not much more disadvantaged in their participation in *communal* religious activity than were non-priestly males. Cultic events at the variety of shrines described or alluded to in the Hebrew Bible, including the Jerusalem temple complex, were generally gender inclusive. For example, although addressed to the collective "you" (masculine), the general stipulations in Deuteronomy (12:12; 16:11, 14) for bringing offerings to the central sanctuary (the temple in Jerusalem) and for keeping festivals include female relatives and servants.[22] The Hannah narrative (1 Samuel 1–2) indicates that women also carried out individual religious acts, such as vows dealing with infertility, at communal shrines.[23] And texts in Deuteronomy (29:11; 31:12) and Joshua (8:35) consider women to be part of the covenant community.[24] Note too that the Tammuz worship castigated by Ezekiel (8:14) included women in a complex of ritual acts at the house of Yahweh.[25] Moreover, because the word *nepeš* ("person") can refer to both females and males, women as well as men are instructed in priestly texts to bring offerings to Yahweh.[26] Also, in Ezra 10:1 the assembly of people joining Ezra in praying and weeping includes women. In Neh 8:2 and 10:28 women are part of the postexilic assembly to which Ezra reads the book of the Torah and which then swears loyalty to God's word. And in Neh 12:43 women rejoice along with the men bringing sacrifices.[27]

Recognizing that women were participants in cultic activities at communal shrines is surely important. Such activities took place at a variety of shrines and high places, in addition to the Jerusalem temple, throughout the land in the period of the monarchy. Indeed, eight of the ten cult places that can be identified archaeologically are communal or public.[28] To consider only public religious activities, however, would be to adopt the perspective of the texts, which focus on communal or state praxis, and to miss religious practices that are not linked to specific structures or installations that can be recognized in the archaeological record. The textual invisibility of most rituals carried out in contexts other than communal ones must not be taken as evidence that religious life in household settings was nonexistent or unimportant. Indeed, household religious practices, especially those of women, were arguably more prominent, in terms of the day-to-day experience of most people, than were extra-household religious activities and cultic events.

How can these difficulties in studying woman and religion in ancient Israel be overcome? In my view, the best way to avoid adopting the perspective of the texts themselves or of the male-dominated Judeo-Christian interpretive tradition is to reconceptualize the topic. Rather than think of studying *women's religion* in the period of the Hebrew Bible, we need to think of studying *women's religious culture.*

CHAPTER TWO

Women's Religious Culture

Before describing our procedures, it is important first to establish what is meant by *religious culture* and then to explain what is meant by *women's* religious culture.

Religious culture in ancient Israel was hardly unitary. Contrary to the perspective of the Hebrew Bible and of most of its interpreters, for much if not all of the period of the Hebrew Bible there was no commonly accepted cultic norm and praxis. The term "Israelite religion" probably does not correspond to any well-defined historical reality; rather, it is an umbrella term for the religions of various groups with different, albeit overlapping, beliefs, activities, liturgies. Ancient Israel had multiple religions.[1] Like those of most premodern peoples, the religions of the Israelites had two interconnected components: (a) a theological one: beliefs in supernatural deities or powers recognized by the group or groups to which people belonged; (b) a behavioral one: appropriate responses to those powers, responses that were meant variously to praise, appease, or somehow manipulate the impact of those divine beings on people's lives.[2]

This broad understanding of religion is best designated as *religious culture*, for it typically involves a material or behavioral element. It acknowledges that religion involves not only belief in one or more supernatural beings but also responses to them. Responses, it is important to note, are not limited to verbal or liturgical modes; they can also be actions or activities, with or without accompanying words. Performative ritual is thus an integral part of religion, not independent of or secondary to beliefs. Moreover, as cross-cultural studies have discovered, the religious lives of women in particular are characterized by non-verbal or non-textual activities.[3] Therefore, using the term *culture* along with *religious* acknowledges the material and behavioral components of women's religious lives.

Religious culture carried out in households and without trained officiants is hardly limited to ancient Israel and other traditional societies. For example, the study of religion in America has recently begun to advocate approaches that focus on what people—the laity—do to "practice" their religion outside of institutional structures. Many researchers now recognize that what people do in their homes as well as in other informal contexts should be taken seriously. Religion is not only a distinct category of experience, often considered sacred or spiritual and as such distinct from the "profane" or mundane. What is often overlooked is that it also can have a dynamic relationship with daily realities and is often manifest in activities, using available cultural forms, that help people negotiate the urgent and immediate needs of their daily existence. Such practices, termed "lived religion" or "religion on the ground," are acknowledged to have enormous social and personal value.[4] They are best studied by engaging social science methods (sociology and anthropology) as well as traditional historical and theological modes of inquiry. In approach as well as conceptualization, the study of lived religion is analogous to this study of religious culture in biblical antiquity.

As for identifying the meaning of the possessive *women's* in women's religious culture, it entails asking whether there are religious practices that are uniquely or exclusively female. Without succumbing to essentialist views about femaleness, the notion of women's religious culture can be considered most relevant with respect to the biological asymmetry of humans. That is, the exclusivity of women's reproductive capacity produced associated religious practices exclusive to women.[5] Indeed, the life processes related to female biology are typically marked, across cultures, in behaviors performed only by women. Such practices are probably the most common of women's religious behaviors.[6] Yet they have been among the least studied, perhaps because they are typically not expressed in texts.

The formation of ritual behaviors in relation to reproduction is a function of the critical place of birth processes in the life cycle and of the life-or-death risks involved at each stage. Giving birth means danger to the life of the mother and of the infant. In biblical antiquity, as many as one in two children failed to live to adulthood; and the average life span of women was significantly shorter than that of men, in part because of the risks of dying in childbirth.[7] Furthermore, the alternative—not having children—meant jeopardizing the viability of the family and even the community. For any premodern agrarian people such as the Israelites, the production of offspring is essential for maintaining the household's food supply and thus its survival, and also for providing care for aging adults.[8] In such a context, infertility, childbirth complications resulting in the death of the mother or child, difficulty in lactation, and high infant mortality rates are constant threats to the durability of the family household.

Women's religious practices can thus be seen as strategies, akin to preventative and restorative medical procedures of the modern world, to intervene with the divine forces believed to impact the well-being of mother and child and to influence them in order to assure their benevolent and protective presence or to avert their destructive powers. The rituals surrounding pregnancy, labor, and birth, along with those securing fertility before pregnancy and those dealing with postpartum lactation, infant care, and circumcision, constitute the religious culture of women more than of men. Some related women's rituals that involve community shrines are biblically visible in certain priestly directives relating to childbirth, menstruation, and women's abnormal genital discharge (Lev 12:2–8; 15:18–33; 18:19; 20:18).[9] But those texts are not comprehensive, nor do they seem relevant for issues beyond the sanctity of the shrine. More important, they are not indicative of a woman's ritual activities in her own household, which is the typical context for women's religious culture.[10]

CHAPTER THREE

An Anthropological Approach

The religious culture of reproduction is only vaguely alluded to, if at all, in the Hebrew Bible; yet it was arguably of central importance to virtually all Israelite women and their families. The Bible may be a poor source for identifying and understanding this culture, but fortunately anthropological approaches can be used to establish the existence of women's religious culture in ancient Israel and to understand its dynamics. Anthropologists who study prehistoric or ahistoric cultures have developed techniques for recovering and reconstructing gendered aspects of those cultures. The virtual silence of the biblical record about the religious culture of Israelite women with respect to reproduction renders that culture similarly ahistoric and calls for similar investigative strategies, which draw on multiple non-textual as well as textual sources.

One advantage of an anthropological approach is that it allows for the inclusion of magic as a legitimate and efficacious aspect of religious behavior. Magic is too often considered occult, quasi-religious, marginal, deviant, primitive, or antireligious in contrast to pure and spiritual religion. This supposed "opposition" between religion and magic is rooted in Western intellectualist biases, reflecting the evolutionary perspectives of late-nineteenth- and early-twentieth-century anthropologists, against modes of thought deemed irrational or superstitious.[1] Malinowski, for example, discusses the "crudity and irrelevance of Magic" while seeing it as a necessary step in the eventual advance to "higher stages of culture."[2]

Biblical scholars, however, continued to be influenced by such views even after anthropologists themselves rejected them. Harsh attitudes toward magic can be found in the mid-twentieth-century works on Israelite religion mentioned above. Fohrer, for example, calls magic "dangerous."[3] Kaufmann acknowledges that Israelites believed in magic and called it idolatrous "heathen wisdom."[4] Consider too the comments of Walther Eichrodt, in his commentary on the book of Ezekiel: "Experienced pastors have expressed their opinions that even in Christian congregations the hidden growth of the weed of magical belief and practice is one of the greatest obstacles to the progress of the message of the gospel and the development of a healthy church life."[5] Such perspectives have been particularly detrimental to evaluating women's religious culture, for the polarization of magic and religion is often associated with gender: religion is considered a higher form and is deemed masculine, whereas debased magic is labeled feminine.[6]

Fortunately, more recent studies no longer see magic and religion as essentially separate, let alone oppositional, categories. When viewed from a contemporary anthropological perspective rather than from traditional evolutionary or theologically oriented approaches, magic is understood to play a vital role in helping people deal with the kind of life–death issues that are resolved or approached in the modern world primarily through medicine and the social sciences. Performing magical ritual acts, either as individuals or through the help of specialists, afforded people some sense of control and thus of mental ease as they confronted the dangers of disease and death. Throughout the ancient world, "health care systems" were integrally related with religious culture.[7] Similarly, concerns for how present behaviors may impact one's future welfare are met today through a wide variety of decision-making "sciences." In premodern societies, prognosticatory procedures or rituals served the same essential and reassuring function of discerning what might happen and then taking appropriate action: manipulating gods or cosmic forces in order to control the outcome of anticipated events. Lacking what modern medicine, psychology, economics, and political science provide, magical practices in biblical antiquity offered the possibility for achieving a sense of control over what happens or might happen to an individual or group. Magic, therefore, should be acknowledged as a valuable and important aspect of religious life for Israelites. If women are particularly implicated in the use or practice of what is deemed magic, then their practices must be understood as religious in nature and must be accordingly recognized and evaluated.

An anthropological approach is also useful in that it involves the use of several different kinds of data—*archaeological*, *textual*, and *ethnographic*. In fact, the multidisciplinary nature of this project, not unlike the integrative approaches to the study of "lived religions" in the modern world, places it within the realm of what anthropologists call *ethnohistory*, a method of understanding the past that is informed by the critical use of ethnographic data and anthropological categories and concepts, as well as archaeology and written remains.[8] The materiality of women's religious culture lends itself to the study of archaeological artifacts; and relevant items recovered from excavations of Syro-Palestinian sites will thus be the starting point for this project. Then the information from documents, including the Bible and other ancient Near Eastern texts, will be related to the evidence from archaeology. And ethnographic data will be consulted in order to provide interpretive possibilities.

Focusing on material remains and the ritual activities that can be associated with them, without primary concern about the attached beliefs in one or another deity, has the added advantage of allowing us to proceed synchronically, without taking into account the changes over the centuries in ancient Israel's beliefs, as it moved from religious diversity to the worship of one god, Yahweh. Particularly because activities themselves, apart from meanings or explanations attached to them, are subject to fewer developmental changes over time, it is possible to consider evidence from the range of Iron Age sites considered Israelite.[9]

The locus for this investigation will be the *family household*. This term is more appropriate than "family" (a term focusing on people) or "domestic unit" (which indicates a domicile), neither of which is inclusive of the other or of the activities and material culture, other than the dwelling, that are part of households. Thus *household* is a more comprehensive and accurate term. It signifies a built environment consisting of persons, their *hardware*—that is, their material culture, including the dwelling and all its associated installations and artifacts—and also their activities.[10]

The household is fundamental to any premodern human society; it can be considered a strategy, participating in and utilizing material culture, to meet the productive and reproductive needs of human beings.[11] In relation to ancient Israel, the "family household," especially in its compound or extended forms, probably coincides with biblical terminology. The phrase *bêt 'āb*, literally "house of the father," occurs frequently in the Hebrew Bible and represents ancient Israel's male-dominated sociopolitical structure.[12] A related phrase, *bêt 'ēm*, literally "house of the mother," also occurs, although it appears less often, notably in texts depicting the internal dynamics of household life.[13] Both these phrases—one from the male perspective, the other from the female—denote the family household.

Whatever the designation, the family household, as for all premodern agrarian societies, was the center of the economic, social, and religious lives of almost all people in ancient Israel. With virtually all of the life activities of a family taking place in the household, its relatively limited activity areas served multiple purposes. Most household spaces served different functions and were used differently by various family members according to age and gender, at various times of the day and seasons of the year. A workplace at certain times of day, for example, could be a social place or a meal place at other times. As such, the household, or some part of its space, could temporarily be the locus of holiness. Analyzing the architecture of Israelite houses thus would not necessarily reveal a specific area for religious activities. To be sure, "cult corners"—secondary usage of space serving other functions—and even a few "cult rooms" have been identified in Iron Age domestic structures at several sites.[14] Such spaces, however, are not statistically significant enough to allow scholars to make generalizations about fixed ritual spaces in households. Ritual acts were conceivably performed in virtually any area of a household. Thus, wherever ritual behaviors took place in household space, that space would have been transformed to sacred space for the duration of the rituals. Holiness can be mediated through charismatic persons and speech; but it can also characterize space—any space—in which performative ritual activities take place.[15]

Many scholars have already pointed to women's religious activities in the family household in their discussions of what they call variously family religion, domestic religion, family-centered religion, home-centered religion, or family cult.[16] However, those studies are problematic in their tendency to assume that the elder male in a family unit controlled the religious behaviors of that unit. Consider, for example, the assertions that "the patriarchal family at worship replicates the pattern of patriarchal society"[17] and that the "father exercised priestly function."[18] Such assumptions can be disputed. Religious activities conceived and carried out by women as well as by men are characteristically part of household life in traditional cultures. Men may not have always been aware of the ritual behaviors of women, but their existence seems certain. Although they rarely leave textual records, the combined evidence from archaeology and ethnography, as well as allusions in texts and information from the records of other ancient Near Eastern peoples, attest to women's household religious activities.

CHAPTER FOUR

Archaeological Evidence

The archaeological remains that can be most directly associated with the rituals of female reproduction are iconographic. Chief among these are the small terracotta figurines, usually eight to fourteen centimeters high, depicting standing women, apparently naked, at least from the waist up. The lower part of the body is not rendered. The descriptive term "pillar-figurine" is usually used to designate these hand-made objects because of the mode of construction of the body: the upper body shows the head, neck, shoulders, arms, hands, and breasts of the woman; but the stylized lower body is in the shape of a pillar that flares slightly at its concave base, thus enabling it to stand. A variant type, usually somewhat larger, has a mold-made head attached to the body.[1] Virtually all of these figurines portray standing women with their hands placed under their breasts, and thus it is likely that they have some relation to the female nurturance of infants.

Such figurines have been widely discussed in the archaeological literature for more than a century.[2] As the titles of many of these studies indicate (e.g., *The Judean Pillar-Figurines and the Archaeology of Asherah*; *Palestinian Figurines in Relation to Certain Goddesses Known through Literature*; *Pillar Figurines of Iron Age Israel and Asherah/Asherim*; *The Cult of Asherah in Ancient Israel and Judah: Evidence for a Hebrew Goddess*), the interpretive interest has focused on the identification of the objects with one or another of the female deities of Canaanite-Israelite culture (Asherah, Anat, or Astarte), or even some great "mother goddess," or nourishing goddess (*dea nutrix*).[3] Even scholars who do not believe that it is possible to ascertain which goddess the figurines represent still tend to assume that they are meant to depict female deities.

But the assumption that the figurines represent a goddess is problematic. Unlike small terra-cotta plaques depicting nude women holding their breasts or other more sophisticated terra-cottas that are found in Syro-Palestinian sites of the Late Bronze and Iron Ages, the pillar-figurines lack the insignia or decoration typically used to represent deities. They wear no crowns and carry no objects that would symbolize divine power, nor do they have any of the elaborate costumes or jewelry that denote the high rank of a deity. In fact, they are often rather crude. Moreover, a significant majority of the figurines were found broken. That feature, in addition to the fact that they are small and that they are made of an ordinary material (clay), suggests that they are not cult figures representing deities but rather are vehicles of magical practice.[4] Such figures are typically used in rituals intended to deal with specific family situations, such as increasing fertility or producing healthy children.[5] It is therefore far more likely that they are votary figures representing human females seeking the aid of a deity—any deity—in pregnancy, birth, and/or lactation.[6] Or, more generally, these objects can be considered metaphors in material form.[7] They are the physical expression of a woman's prayers for fertility and successful lactation; as tangible and visible objects, they represent what women seek.

But even if the figurines are meant to represent a deity, the focus on identifying who that goddess might be detracts from a consideration of their function. Whether they represent a particular goddess, or the human supplicants of any deity, or perhaps even both, they surely were part of women's religious culture. They were small, relatively inexpensive items; women did not have to be wealthy or be members of elite families to obtain them, as is indicated by where they have been discovered by archaeologists. Indeed, it is their context that indicates their role in women's religious lives. The connection of the pillar-figurines with women's culture is weakly indicated by the fact that there are no equivalent male terracottas and strongly by where they are typically found.

Hundreds of these figures appear in tenth- to sixth-century BCE contexts from over one hundred sites west and east of the Jordan River, some forty to forty-five of those sites probably in the territory of the kingdom of Judah.[8] They are virtually absent from communal cultic contexts. By far the most common find-spot for the figurines is within the household, whether in rooms, courtyards, silos or pits, and cisterns.[9] Some of those locations are clearly secondary, perhaps the result of the discarding of broken figurines. Others are part of roof collapses in household space and may represent second-floor or roof usage—both the second story and the roof were used for various household activities, including cultic or religious ones, in the four-room houses that were the characteristic Israelite dwellings of the Iron Age.[10] Tombs, which are also common find-spots, may be considered household space in that family tombs, as abodes for deceased ancestors, are extensions of the kinship component of the family household.[11]

Based on the quantity of objects in relation to excavated domestic structures, it is possible to calculate the presence of at least one figurine per household.[12] Whether in households or tombs, these figurines were presumably endowed with sympathetic magic properties; they were meant to secure fertility, safe childbirth, and/or adequate lactation. They may or may not have been connected to a particular deity; but their most likely function, because of what they depict and where they are found, would have been to help women with the concerns of reproduction. Such an interpretation is supported by the fact that not only are these terra-cotta figurines recovered from households but also that they are often found as part of assemblages containing other artifacts that are clearly related to women's concerns with respect to the reproductive process.

One such artifact is another iconographic one. Small statues as well as other depictions of the Egyptian dwarf god Bes are also typically found in households and tombs and were incontrovertibly part of women's religious culture. Perhaps the best-known representations of Bes, because they accompany controversial renderings of Yahweh and Asherah along with a tree of life, are the drawings on a large eighth-century BCE storage jar from Kuntillet ʿAjrud, a site in the northeast Sinai peninsula that was probably an Israelite outpost.[13] But numerous small figurines of the god have also been discovered in household contexts; and representations appear on many other objects, including amulets, seals, scarabs, and ceramic appliqués.[14] In fact, Bes artifacts are found often enough in Syro-Palestinian sites to suggest that his popularity extended throughout Israelite territory in the Iron II period and even later.[15] Moreover, the Bes amulets are not simply Egyptian imports; discovery of several molds at Palestinian sites attests to indigenous production.[16]

Evidence from names (onomastic data) also attests to Bes's presence. Many names of people in the biblical period have theophoric elements; that is, they incorporate the name of a deity. Most such names in the Hebrew Bible and on Iron Age inscriptions are Yahwistic, for they use the name of Israel's god, or a shortened form of it. For example, the name Joshua is theophoric; in Hebrew it is *yĕhôšūaʿ* (Yehoshua), which means "Yahweh saves." Surprisingly, names with *bs* (Bes) elements are among the few non-Yahwistic theophoric names of the Iron II period.[17]

The popularity of Bes can be attributed to his role, known from Egyptian sources, as guardian of women in childbirth and of newborns. By the first millennium BCE in Egypt, Bes was considered a major life force, with his grotesque figure used to ward off evil demons and sustain the life of new mother and child.[18] Similar functions can be conjectured for the Bes images found in tombs and households, sometimes along with pillar-figurines, in Iron Age Palestine.[19] Whether those who used them were consciously invoking the god Bes or were simply appropriating what was considered a powerful apotropaic image cannot be ascertained. However, the latter is certainly possible, if not probable, for visual symbols can maintain their power but not necessarily their attendant "explanation" when they migrate across cultures.[20] Thus the use of Bes amulets did not necessarily mean the worship of that deity.

A good example of that process, in which symbols migrate across cultures but in so doing lose their original theological meaning, is represented by another artifact sometimes found in household cultic assemblages: the *wedjat* or eye symbol. To this day such objects, which were originally meant to signify the eye of the Egyptian god Horus, are found all over the Mediterranean world to keep away the "evil eye." An eye symbol appears atop a pyramid on the back of the dollar bill in U.S. currency, and the modern Rx symbol used for prescriptions may be a stylized eye echoing the ancient symbol for healing. In Egyptian antiquity and ever since, the eye image has been a protective symbol, thought to ward off illness and promote healing. Yet it is unlikely that current users of the eye symbol believe in Horus, and the same is probably true for non-Egyptian users of the image in antiquity.

Thus, whether those who used Bes images or *wedjat* representations believed in the Egyptian god or not, there can be little doubt that these images helped women cope with the risks of motherhood and thus were part of women's religious culture. Perhaps the images of the dwarf figure Bes were understood to ward off the dangers of *negative* supernatural forces, thus complementing the pillar-figurines, which may have been meant to invoke the *positive* benefits of divine blessings.[21]

One other kind of artifact, albeit quite rare, also suggests concerns with reproduction. In two different structures in ninth- to eighth-century BCE strata at Beer-sheba, a miniature bed, or "couch model," as the excavators call it, was discovered together with a pillar-figurine and a miniature lamp.[22] Lamps will be discussed below. But at this point, the tiny (ca. seven centimeters high and eleven centimeters long) bed models are noteworthy, for perhaps they are meant to signify the place of copulation or of giving birth, or both. Together with the pillar-figurines and lamps, they have been interpreted as a collection of items belonging to women and used to ensure fertility, safe childbirth, and successful lactation.[23]

The presence of pillar-figurines, Bes images, eye images, and even an occasional miniature bed in household groupings of artifacts is a good indicator that certain household areas were sites of the religious culture of women and were associated with their reproductive concerns. Many of the other items in these assemblages—especially small lamps, knife blades, jewelry, amulets, shells, and perhaps even rattles—that do not seem intrinsically symbolic or religious in nature can be similarly interpreted. Textual and ethnographic sources provide invaluable information to support this reading of those other items recovered by archaeology, while also offering a glimpse of other rituals relating to the reproductive process.

CHAPTER FIVE

Textual Sources

Documents from ancient Israel (specifically, the Hebrew Bible) and from surrounding cultures are also important resources. As already indicated, the Hebrew Bible has no prescriptive cultic texts relating directly to female reproduction and infant care (except for the purification rituals in Leviticus specified for the communal shrine). Several narrative and poetic texts, however, contain indirect allusions to acts or utterances that were arguably part of women's religious culture.

With respect to fertility, several petitionary prayers are mentioned. Some are uttered by males (for example, Abraham in Gen 15:2 and 20:17–18; and Isaac in Gen 25:21). But women are also depicted, directly or indirectly, as seeking fertility through religious activity. Hannah prays for an end to her barrenness (1 Sam 1:10–11), and a prayer is implicit in the hopeful message that Samson's mother receives from Yahweh in relation to her infertility (Judg 13:3). These texts make no mention of accompanying ritual, yet they do not preclude the performance of ritual acts to accompany or complement the verbal petitions. Except for the Hannah episode, which involves a formal vow as well as a prayer and which may therefore have necessitated a communal cultic site,[1] a household context is implied.[2] In addition, practices such as eating certain plant substances as a means for promoting fertility are known from other ancient Near Eastern sources. One Babylonian text is a veritable pharmaceutical manual, listing plants to be taken for various aspects of impotency and infertility; others refer to the "plant of becoming pregnant" and the "plant of giving birth," both thought to end infertility and promote conception.[3] The use of the enigmatic mandrake roots of Gen 30:14–17, which seem to have something to do with Leah's fertility, can be considered a household magical act performed to promote fertility.[4]

The rituals of childbirth itself, in which midwives or other women are in attendance, are perhaps visible in the red thread tied around one of Tamar's twin sons (Gen 38:28–30) by the midwife. The narrative describes the thread as an identifying marker, but its use may reflect a set of practices involving the apotropaic character of strands of dyed yarn, with both their red color and the fact that they are bound on the infant's hand having magical protective powers.[5] Both Mesopotamian and Hittite texts support such an interpretation; in the former, a red thread provides protection for the mother, and in the latter, the red thread keeps evil from harming the child.[6]

Another relevant biblical text is Ezek 16:4, which refers to three procedures—washing the newborn, rubbing it with salt, and swaddling it—performed on a baby at birth after the umbilical cord is cut:

1. The *washing* of an infant was probably a ritual meant to assure the safety and health of the newborn. The word used for this (*lĕmišʿi*) appears only once in the Hebrew Bible and is related to an Aramaic word *sʿy*, meaning "to daub, smear."[7] Thus the NRSV translation "to cleanse" does not quite capture the meaning of the Hebrew. The term does not refer simply to bathing the newborn, although rinsing away the placental materials may have been a preliminary step; rather, it may involve the spreading of a protective ointment over the infant.

2. *Rubbing* a baby *with salt* was similarly protective. Although salt sometimes represents danger or destruction in the Bible, it can also signify vitality (as in several cultic texts: e.g., Lev 2:13 and Num 18:19). And it was thought to have had medicinal qualities: it could heal or sustain life, as in 2 Kgs 2:21–22, where salt in the water prevents miscarriage.[8]

3. *Wrapping* a newborn baby in cords or cloths was also meant to keep it from harm. The NRSV "wrapped in cloths" obscures the fact that the Hebrew uses only a verb (*ḥtl*), which means "to wrap." But the same root appears in the noun "cloths" (*ḥittûl*, translated "bandage" in the NRSV) in Ezek 30:21 in a magico-medical context. And note that in Luke 2:7, in reference to the birth of Jesus, the Greek term for swaddling, translated "wrapped . . . in bands of cloth," is derived from a noun meaning "cloth bands." Thus the verb does indicate wrapping snugly with cloths, or swaddling. This procedure, performed by many peoples even today on a newborn for the first week or so of its life, may help the baby stay warm until its own internal thermostat functions properly. It thus contributes to keeping a newborn safe and well. It is no wonder that it was considered a protective

measure in traditional societies, in which neonatal death was attributed to malevolent forces.

That all these procedures can be considered apotropaic actions that were part of women's ritual culture will be further affirmed when one considers the ethnographic data.

Another text provides evidence that women kept lamps burning in their households for apotropaic purposes. The "strong woman"[9] (*'ēšet ḥayil*) of Proverbs 31 keeps a light burning continuously (v. 18), even though she herself is not awake all night (v. 15). If the lamp had no pragmatic value during the dark hours, perhaps it was necessary for the safety of her children, an interpretation supported by the fact that lamp imagery in several other biblical passages is connected with protection. In Prov 6:20–23, parental guidance is seen as lamplight that protects offspring from danger; this passage also alludes to protective amulets worn, day and night, around the necks of children. Job 18:5–6 relates the downfall of the wicked to the extinguishing of the lights (and thus of divine protection?) in their abode; and Job 29:3 likens divine protection to a lamp. Also, 2 Kgs 8:19 suggests the eternal protectiveness of a lamp for the Davidic dynasty and for Judah.

Note too that across cultures light represents well-being and safety in contrast to the dangers of darkness. In this respect, remember that lamps—especially special miniature ones—are typical items in household cultic assemblages and probably served protective (as well as light-giving) functions in those contexts.

Other treatments of the newborn—naming it and, if it is a male child, circumcising it—should also be considered part of women's religious culture. With respect to name-giving, women outnumber men as name-givers in the Hebrew Bible; they are depicted as pronouncing the newborn's name in 62 percent of the name-giving events. Often other women, presumably those helping with the birth, are part of the naming ritual, as for Obed's birth in Ruth 4:14–17[10] and perhaps Ichabod's in 1 Sam 4:20–21. In some instances, both parents name the child: Seth by Eve and Adam, Gershom by Zipporah and Moses, Benjamin by Rachel and Jacob. Because the woman is the first to name the child in each of these cases, the few instances of men naming children may be the result of the male narrative perspective, which attributes to the father the function of name-giving when the names may have actually been given by the mother.[11] In any case, naming a child can be construed as a ritual act that was usually part of women's religious culture.[12] Because a name in the biblical world was not simply a means of identification but rather signified the essence of a person,[13] the anthroponymic (name-giving) process meant establishing the vitality of a new life.

Finally, infant circumcision is likely to have originated as an apotropaic act carried out by women. The strange and cryptic narrative of the circumcision of Gershom by Zipporah (Exod 4:24–26), however else it is to be understood, portrays a mother performing a rite of ritual expiation or purification on her firstborn son,[14] At the least, a female paradigm for sustaining life is provided by Zipporah's deed; at the most, an ancient ritual specialty of women, perhaps originating among the Midianites, is implied.[15]

Documents from other Near Eastern cultures provide evidence more directly related to the iconographic and artifactual materials than does the Hebrew Bible. For example, Egyptian texts describe the manufacture of amulets that would drive away hostile spirits threatening a newborn baby.[16] Such amulets often contained spells to ward off disease, assure safe childbirth, and/or secure an ample supply of mother's milk. An example of such a spell, preserved on papyrus, reads, "To make a protection for a child on the day of its birth."[17] Even the amulet or object itself, without a magico-medical text, would be sufficient to secure protective benefits.[18]

Egyptian texts also refer to certain kinds of jewelry—including pendants, shells, beads, rings, and scarabs—that were thought to have apotropaic powers.[19] One such text mentions casting a spell over a "pellet of gold, forty beads, a cornelian seal-stone" and hanging them around the neck of an infant to drive away demons thought to cause fever.[20] The kind of jewelry mentioned in such texts includes items that are part of the artifact assemblages that are found with pillar-figurines and/or Bes images at Israelite sites. These items are often described somewhat neutrally as "items of personal adornment" in the excavation reports of Syro-Palestinian sites. But it is quite possible that many of them were magico-medical amulets that were part of women's religious culture. The power of these shiny items to protect the wearer may be a function of the way they reflect light; like lamplight, they keep the dangers of darkness at bay.

Similar information about women's religious culture is found in Mesopotamian, Canaanite, and Anatolian texts and iconography.[21] These sources indicate that both lamps and apotropaic jewelry were used to ward off the powers of Lamashtu, Lilith, and other demonic beings thought to be particularly dangerous to pregnant or nursing women and to infants.[22] Lamashtu was the most feared of all female Mesopotamian demons; it was believed that she was particularly menacing to women during parturition and to children while they were suckling. Lilith was a Mesopotamian storm demon with many of the same qualities as Lamashtu; she appears once in the Hebrew Bible, in a prophetic oracle portraying her as inhabiting a spooky region of infertility and death (Isa 34:14). She endured into postbiblical Jewish and Islamic folklore as Adam's first wife or as a demon threatening pregnant women and their infants.

Ancient Lamashtu reliefs from Mesopotamia sometimes include lamps among their apotropaic symbols. Many texts instruct women to wear certain kinds of amuletic jewelry or braided cords of dried wool and to perform rituals accompanied by incantations to ward off danger during pregnancy or at birth; and special stones or shells were used to protect pregnant women.[23] The Lamashtu charms from the Canaanite city of Ugarit similarly were used to protect women during pregnancy, childbirth, and lactation.[24] Texts from Anatolia, which indicate specific words to be recited at childbirth, also allude to ritual acts and objects.[25]

Postbiblical Jewish texts, notably Talmudic ones far too numerous to examine here, also attest to a lively involvement of women in magical practices meant to protect them and their offspring. They reveal a belief that demonic powers, including the evil eye, could adversely affect a woman's attempt to conceive and to bear a healthy child. Many of these passages attack women for illicit magical practices, thereby indicating that women indeed engaged in such ritual behaviors in the rabbinic period. But not all these texts are negative. For example, the procedures mentioned in Ezek 16:4 were deemed so important by the rabbis that they were expressly permitted even when performing them might violate the Sabbath.[26] Such texts indicate considerable continuity between practices of the Israelites and those of postbiblical Judaism. Consequently, they suggest that many of the customs mentioned in ancient Jewish literature go back to the biblical period, even if the Bible is silent about them.

In addition to references in the Talmud, a small but important subset of the corpus of inscriptions of late antiquity consists of incantations used as amulets by women to help secure their fertility or protect their health or that of their children.[27] And inscribed *lamellae*—amulets made of metals, gemstones, or perishable materials and found widely in the Roman world—were used by Jews in antiquity, including by women seeking success and protection in their reproductive roles.[28] A typical amuletic text was Exod 22:26—"No woman in your land shall miscarry or be barren."[29] Such customs have survived into the modern world, as ethnographers investigating the behaviors surrounding reproduction among Middle Eastern women have discovered.

CHAPTER SIX

Ethnographic Data

Observational information from existing cultures, along with the Bible and other ancient Near Eastern documents, has long been used for interpreting archaeological remains in order to reconstruct life in biblical antiquity and to postulate its human dynamics. Although the legitimacy of doing so is sometimes challenged, largely because of the enormous chronological distance between cultures being compared, ethnography is invaluable if used cautiously and in conjunction with other sources.[1] Indeed, it would be virtually impossible to interpret archaeological remains from Syro-Palestinian sites and to understand many aspects of daily life in biblical antiquity without the use of ethnographic data—especially from cultures from the same geographical region as ancient Israel or from cultures descended from biblical communities.

Ethnographic data from these cultures indicate a rich set of customs meant to bring fertility and health to a woman of childbearing age, to protect her and the infant at delivery, and to welcome the newborn. Wherever travelers and anthropologists have looked, they have discovered and recorded a wealth of materials relating to women's experience of reproduction and motherhood. These customs combine magical and medical practices and are clearly within the domain of what is considered religion by their practitioners. Ritual behaviors are prescribed in written documents: devotional literature, religious treatises, remedy books, mid-wifery guides, collections of charm texts, obstetrical manuals, and pharmacopoeia. They are also preserved in oral traditions: legends, songs, stories, maxims, and folklore. They specify practices for every phase of the reproductive process: fertility/barrenness, abortion/miscarriage, pregnancy, birthing, welcoming the newborn, circumcision, nursing, naming. The ubiquity and abundance of such behaviors make it inconceivable that women in any premodern society would have lacked such rituals. Their presence even in societies in which women have access to medical attention attests to their enduring importance as cultural practice in women's lives.

The ethnographic materials are far too vast to review here.[2] Rather, examples relevant to practices visible in the archaeological and textual data from the biblical world will be given. They are all household practices meant to assure maternal and infant well-being and, often through the same ritual, preclude difficulties or death.

One of the most common practices in many Middle Eastern countries, among Muslims, Christians, and Jews alike, is the use of eye images or other amulets to ward off the evil eye,[3] an apotropaic act that can be related to the ancient use of the *wedjat* eye symbols or of Bes images. Garnett reports the use of shiny metal to protect young children from disaster, which is symbolized as the "evil eye":

> *Ajin rah*, the evil eye, is as much dreaded by the Jews as by the Christians and Moslems of the east, and their charms and antidotes against it partake, for the most part, of similar character. Little bands of gold and silver are often fastened to the caps of children.[4]

And Kurdish Jewish women are known to have worn silver-threaded, embroidered amulets, made by women who were specialists in such crafts, during pregnancy and childbirth to protect the wearer from danger.[5] All these practices recall the presence of shiny metallic, glass, or gemstone items in household or tomb assemblages likely associated with women's religious culture.

Another custom, which may be relevant to the presence of iron blades in those assemblages, was widely practiced by Jews in Europe, North Africa, Bulgaria, Syria, and Afghanistan.[6] Women in those communities hired a professional exorcist, who symbolically used a knife blade to deal with demons. And Moroccan Jewish women kept a vigil around a new mother and her infant, while an iron blade was brandished (usually by the father, outside of the birthing room) in order to keep Lilith away from the child. These actions recall not only the blades of household assemblages but also the way Bes was thought to wave a sword or knife to avert evil and protect mothers.[7] The fact that Talmudic sages warned against using iron as protective of women in childbirth thereby attests to its use for such purposes in the rabbinic era, if not before.

Two practices of Osmanli (Turkish Muslim) women—the wearing of red kerchiefs or veils at childbirth and placing a red cap on the newborn[8]—are both protective acts reminiscent of the red thread mentioned in the Tamar narrative as well as of the red threads used as protection for mothers and children according to Hittite and Mesopotamian texts. Noteworthy too is the practice, among Albanian Muslims and Moroccan Berbers, for women attending a birth to keep a fire or candle burning continuously near a newborn and its mother, lest supernal beings bring evil.[9] This custom supports the possibility that the lamps found in Israelite household and tomb assemblages and mentioned in Proverbs 31 had similar functions.

Another group of traditions, found in many Middle Eastern communities, corresponds directly to the information in Ezekiel 16 and rabbinic texts.[10] Midwives in early-twentieth-century Syria and Palestine washed a newborn with a mixture of salt and oil and then swaddled it, as did Muslim women in Iran. Bulgarian wisewomen or village "witches" bathed and salted an infant and smeared it with an oily poultice. And in South Macedonia, the baby's first experience outside the womb was being submerged in a bath of salted water and then wrapped in special garments.

Ethnography also establishes that women were especially skilled in invoking the dead in service of the living. As recently as the 1980s elderly Middle Eastern Jewish women living in Jerusalem were found to have a special relationship with deceased ancestors.[11] They petitioned, visited, and negotiated with dead ancestors, who could be saints or biblical figures as well as biological parents or grandparents. They talked to them, often at the graves of relatives or at the tombs of saints or biblical figures such as the matriarchs or even Eve. These elderly women often lit candles (=lamps?) as part of their relationship with ancestral spirits. Their chief reasons for performing such rituals were to secure fertility for daughters or granddaughters, to request protection for those women during pregnancy and childbirth, and to enlist their aid in safeguarding the health and souls of unborn and newborn children. Such activities may be analogous to some functions of female necromancers in the biblical period and perhaps also to the presence of lamps and pillar-figurines in Iron Age tombs.

A similar custom, involving a red thread as well as a tomb, involves pregnant women. To this very day, or at least until the political situation made it impossible, pregnant women travel to Rachel's Tomb, the traditional burial place of the matriarch, near Bethlehem. They wind a scarlet thread around the tomb seven times (seven is a symbolic holy number), which affords it mystical protective powers. They then tie the thread around their neck or wrist to ward off all kinds of dangers. Women in Diaspora

Jewish communities sometimes request a traveler to Israel to wind a thread around that tomb and bring it back to them to wear during pregnancy or childbirth.[12] Or one can even order on the internet a red string, which has been properly wound around the tomb, from a religious organization in Israel called "The Faithful of Rachel's Tomb."[13] Because Rachel overcomes barrenness herself and then dies in childbirth (Gen 29:31; 30:1–24; 35:16–21), she is deemed in Jewish tradition to be especially receptive to the prayers of barren women. For millennia, Jews have made pilgrimages to Rachel's Tomb, considered the third-holiest shrine in the Land of Israel.

This tiny sample of the ritual customs of recent and even contemporary Mediterranean cultures bears witness to women's religious practices, in households and at tombs, with many features that resemble those of biblical antiquity. Just as important is the fact that the ethnographic sources uniformly show that the participants in these rituals, which are understood by their practitioners to be religious in nature, are—not surprisingly—mainly women. Male relatives are sometimes peripherally involved; but the major players, in addition to the expectant or new mother and the infant, are other women. These include female family members, especially mothers or mothers-in-law, and neighboring women, like the *šĕkēnôt* (female neighbors) mentioned in Ruth 4 and alluded to in 1 Samuel 4. In addition, professional women—midwives, wisewomen, witches, herbalists, and others—frequently had significant roles in the religious culture surrounding female biological processes.

CHAPTER SEVEN

Discussion

Although the artifacts of Israelite sites are silent about who used them, the pillar-figurines and other objects in household assemblages are compelling indications of the involvement of women in ritual behaviors relating to maternity. Biblical texts allude to aspects of a ritual culture surrounding reproduction, and other ancient Near Eastern sources mention such practices directly. The ethnographic evidence corresponds to many of the archaeological and ethnographic materials. Taken together, all these data attest to a woman's religious culture that would have been part of Israelite households in the Iron Age. Moreover, although evidence for the verbal accompaniments of religious acts does not survive in the Bible, postbiblical Jewish texts as well as Hittite and Mesopotamian documents preserve prayers and incantations to be used in relation to women's reproductive processes[1] and make it likely that Israelite women similarly recited or chanted standard texts. Much of their religious culture met needs that today would be considered clinical or medical; but in antiquity women's household religious acts, perhaps accompanied by appropriate prayers and incantations, were clearly religious.

We can now interrogate that culture for information about women's lives. To do so means first putting aside two related and common assumptions about social organization and religious life in premodern societies so that the importance of the religious culture of the household can be better appreciated.

The first assumption to be challenged is that the household is *tertiary*, as it has been identified in studies of the overall social organization of ancient Israel.[2] Our familiarity with the Bible has unfortunately obscured the centrality of the household, even for archaeologists. Biblical narratives and prophecies focus largely on tribal, national, or state interests; and archaeology has let the agendas of the texts set the agendas of the digs, which until recently have sought to recover evidence of ethnicities and kingdoms rather than of the household units in which most people lived. As anthropologists have amply demonstrated, the family household in premodern agrarian societies is the place where the "most primary functions of society take place."[3]

This would certainly have been true throughout the Iron Age. Even during the monarchic period, most people lived in agrarian settlements, whether they were small rural villages and hamlets or somewhat larger walled villages and towns; few lived in settlements that were truly urban.[4] Social scientists have shown that the urban segment of agrarian societies was never more than a small percentage of the total. Russian records, for example, indicate that even in the late eighteenth century, only 3 percent of the total population was urban.[5] The common translation of the biblical word *'îr* into English as "city" is thus misleading. Note that *mibṣārîm* ("fortified towns") is the most frequent biblical specification of *'îr*.[6] Most biblical "cities" were in fact small settlements that bore no resemblance to what we mean by "city" in the modern world.

In the rural agrarian context of ancient Israel, the household, as described above, was the central economic and social location of most Israelites. And successful reproduction was essential to household life, especially because of the dominant, labor-intensive agrarian regimes.[7] That is, without the labor of older children, the work that had to be done at certain times of the year, especially at harvest, could not be satisfactorily accomplished; and even young children were enlisted sporadically for various household tasks. Furthermore, grown children were essential for the care of adults who survived into their senior years. Thus, in light of masses of data from the anthropology of ancient and even contemporary premodern societies, it seems much more accurate to acknowledge the family household as the *primary*, not the tertiary, social unit of the Israelites.

The second assumption to be contested concerns the meaning and value of women's religious behaviors and is related to the problem, mentioned above, of masculinized approaches to religion. Women's behaviors are too often evaluated in terms of our experiences in Western Judeo-Christian tradition. Consequently, that which is masculine is considered inherently powerful and/or prestigious, with women's activities seen as supportive and secondary, thereby being trivialized or marginalized. To put it another way, formal structures of religious life controlled by male clergy tend to be viewed as more important or more legitimate than the informal but no-less-structured aspects of religious life practiced by females.[8] Furthermore, the specific behaviors typical of women's praxis are automatically considered less valuable than abstract formulations. Even feminist scholars find it difficult to let go of the notion that "the more abstract and transcendent something is, the better it is."[9]

Such attitudes must be recognized as culture-bound constructions of Western religious studies and not as a reflection of the "lived" reality of other peoples, or even of people today, as those studying "religion on the ground" in America are discovering. We must abandon them if we are to understand and appreciate women's religious culture in biblical antiquity or, for that matter, in any society at any time. This means rejecting the notion that male roles in formal organizations represent a "higher form of religious experience."[10] Instead, we must acknowledge that the informal household religious culture of women involved technical behaviors just as dependent on specialized knowledge as were the formal structures that depended on priestly expertise. Assertions that household cultic activity meant (a) male priestly functions and (b) no specialized cult personnel[11] must also be rejected. Similarly, claims mentioned above about the patriarchal family with the father as the chief priestly figure must be abandoned or modified in light of all the evidence for women's household religious practices. It is no longer conscionable to ignore or deprecate women's cultic practices.

With those cautions in mind, the dynamic and essential role of women's religious culture in ancient Israel can be examined. Several important points emerge:

1. The behaviors described above all represent the existence of a substantial body of knowledge. Rituals by definition are stereotyped behaviors that must be learned from experts, and ritual activities involving materials and artifacts depend on the knowledge of specialists who prepare the materials in prescribed ways and carry out the acts in the same way each time. If rituals are to be efficacious in influencing higher powers to produce the described outcome, fixed ritual procedures must be scrupulously observed.[12]

Women's religious culture therefore entailed the services of experts in the overlapping physiological and material aspects of the reproductive process. These experts were often the female relatives or neighbors of a woman seeking or experiencing pregnancy and childbirth. Older women served as mentors, transmitting their knowledge to their younger relatives or neighbors. Sometimes the outside expertise of professionals was sought, and the Bible preserves evidence of at least four such groups:

a. **Midwives**. Midwifery is surely among the earliest and most ubiquitous specialized functions in human society, and it is likely that Israelites routinely enlisted the aid of such specialists. The matriarch Rachel is attended by a midwife (Gen 35:17), and a midwife—the one who ties a "crimson thread" around the wrist of one of the newborns—is present at the delivery of Tamar's two sons (Gen 38:28).[13] Midwives are likely the women who are present at the birth of Ichabod in 1 Sam 4:20.[14] And Puah and Shiphrah are the two heroic midwives who defy Pharaoh's orders at the beginning of the exodus narrative (Exod 1:15–21).[15] Prayers and incantations are ubiquitous aspects of the practice of midwifery in traditional cultures; that is, midwives must be recognized as religious as well as medical professionals.

b. **Necromancers**. As noted above, ethnographic evidence indicates that older women are often the ones who enlist the aid of the dead to achieve fertility or to protect mothers and infants; and the prominence of women, such as the medium of Endor (1 Sam 28:7–25), as necromancers in the Hebrew Bible may be relevant in this regard.[16] The presence of so many pillar-figurines in tombs may indicate their use there by elderly women engaged in necromancy—in mediating between the living and their dead ancestors—in the service of their daughters' fertility.[17] Moreover, the enigmatic biblical *tĕrapîm* (teraphim—sometimes rendered "household gods" or "idols" by the NRSV) are arguably statuettes representing ancestors. Teraphim figure prominently in the narratives of two biblical women: Rachel (Gen 31:19, 34) and Tamar (1 Sam 19:13).[18] In any case, the practice of necromancy by both men and women is strongly condemned in Leviticus (19:31; 20:6, 27) and Deuteronomy (18:11), and even the narrative of the woman of Endor may be a foil to discredit Saul.[19] Yet communing with the dead apparently was important for many Israelite women.

c. **Sorcerers**. Another possible specialist in reproductive ritual was the "sorcerer" (*mĕkaššĕpâ*). Sorcerers are the only ones among the catalog of forbidden cultic professionals (Deut 18:10–12) for whom female practitioners are specifically mentioned (in Exod 22:18 and Isa 57:3). The negative biblical perspective on these professionals is perhaps because they were expert at preventing conception or inducing abortion, both procedures abhorrent to clan ideology encouraging procreation.[20] Sorcerers may also have been, more generally, health care consultants.[21] Either way, they are viewed negatively in biblical texts, perhaps because of the insistence that Yahweh is the sole resource for dealing with what we would consider medical problems.

d. **Diviners**. A strong anti-divination passage in Ezek 13:17–23 is addressed to a group of female prophets. These women "sew bands on all wrists" and engage in other rituals involving veils; and their activities also seem to involve grain (barley) and bread. Careful examination of the language indicates that it reflects divinatory activities and incantations associated with pregnancy and childbearing.[22] Ezekiel's distress about these practitioners, of course, indicates their existence, if not their popularity, within the diversity of beliefs and practices of Israelites in the Iron Age.

These professional specialists, all engaged in what can be considered religious activity, drew on a corpus of information that was likely passed from one practitioner to the next in guilds, a term that can be used loosely as a designation for groups of professionals who provide similar services.[23] The silence of the Bible about such associations does not mean that they were not present among the Israelites; for informal organizations of women with technical expertise in birthing or healing, for example, are found widely, including among the Hittites and in Mesopotamia, where certain female religious functionaries served as midwives or even as experts in bringing about abortion.[24] Ethnographic information shows that the services of such women, whether professionals or "volunteers," would have afforded them prestige and status within their profession and for the women they helped, in much the same way that male cultic professionals experienced the regard of their communities.

2. Although some practices of the religious culture of reproduction—such as using amulets or herbal preparations for themselves and their infants—involved the behaviors of individual women as part of their daily routine, many others were carried out by groups of female kin and neighbors. The performance of religious rituals surrounding the intimate circumstances of childbirth typically creates solidarity among those present. Such bonds among women, along with those created by women carrying out economic

activities together,[25] mean the formation of informal networks of women. These connections among women would have been invaluable for dealing with the inevitable economic or medical difficulties requiring the assistance of one household to another. In fact, such informal women's networks may have constituted an important mediating group that helped forge households into the larger kin groups, or *mišpāḥôt*, which extended aid across household boundaries.[26] Indeed, women in traditional and even contemporary cultures are the ones with the kinds of ties to each other that characteristically provide material and emotional support in times of war, illness, or famine.[27] Women's religious culture was just one manifestation of the complex set of informal female social bonds that contributed to the survival of Israelite families and communities and that afforded women the same kind of satisfaction, although less visible and little noticed, that males achieve from exercising formal leadership roles.

3. The religious culture of women in households was not concerned with matters of life and death as abstract problems. Rather, their concerns with life and death were immediate and direct. Their ritual praxis was focused on the welfare of

themselves and their families.[28] To say that women's religious activities were a strategy for dealing with the "minor distresses of everyday life"[29] is to demean profoundly important and meaningful aspects of their lives. Women were practitioners of specialized behaviors that were essential for the creation and maintenance of new life. Female power and value, and a concomitant sense of self-worth, are typical of group-oriented societies, such as ancient Israel, in which women's roles as the creators and sustainers of life are especially critical.[30]

Insofar as household religious culture dealing with reproduction was almost exclusively female, it meant that women controlled vital socioreligious functions. Such functions are deemed marginal only when seen from the top down, from the perspective of elite, male-dominated, formal structures. But they are central to a society when seen from the bottom up, from the informal household setting in which virtually all Israelites lived. Thus, women's religious culture would have empowered them as major religious actors in their households. Indeed, in their access to the supernatural in the religious culture of the households, women may have experienced power that countered other, male-specific, cultural forms.[31]

4. Finally, the existence of women's informal groups and of expert female professionals raises the whole question of social hierarchies. Like male groups, female groups and guilds, even informal ones, have their own structures and hierarchies. Older women and specialists would have held authoritative positions within the culture of birthing. In other words, women's religious culture involves women's hierarchical structures, separate from those of men.

Because analogous women's structures, each with its own hierarchies, were present in other aspects of Israelite life—such as musical performance[32] and the production of food and textiles[33]—the conventional wisdom about male dominance in pervasive hierarchical structures affecting all domains of human interaction can be disputed. If one aspect of "patriarchy" is that "men monopolize or dominate all the roles and pursuits that society most values, such as religious leadership or economic power,"[34] then the vital role of women's religious, social, and economic activities in ancient Israelite households subverts that notion. Power in premodern societies was hardly monolithic or unitary; rather, there were multiple loci of power, with women as well as men shaping societies.[35]

The gendered spheres of Israelite society, as grounded in household life, are thus best considered complementary rather than hierarchical.[36] This reconstruction of the dynamics of women's religious culture supports the notion, to continue further the anthropological rather than historic perspective necessary for a more sympathetic reading of the past, that Israelite society was organized heterarchically rather than hierarchically. Hierarchy is not the only mode of social complexity and should not be privileged as such. When women as well as men control aspects of economic and religious life, as was the case for agrarian Israelite households, well-developed and complex lateral and parallel relationships are formed.[37] The concept of *heterarchy*—developed by anthropologists, who were dissatisfied with the shortcomings of traditional evolutionary models of sociocultural complexity, as a model for understanding premodern complex societies—fits such complexity.[38]

The term *heterarchy* signifies an organizational pattern in which "each element possesses the potential of being unranked (relative to other elements) or ranked in different ways depending on systemic requirements."[39] As such, it allows for systems to be perceived as related to each other laterally rather than vertically. In such a conceptualization, women's activities are sub-systems, each with its own rankings, privileges, and statuses, with some women exercising meaningful leadership and dominance vis-à-vis other women in the system. Women's systems, together with those of men, are constituent systems of heterarchical complexities.

Women's religious culture, like other components of Israelite household life that can be identified as female activities, would have contributed to such heterarchical complexity. In this respect, it is interesting to go back to the Garnett volumes quoted at the beginning. Garnett's editor, in reviewing all the data she provided, observed that in many instances "acknowledged supremacy was accorded to women"; and he even went so far as to suggest that the "reverse of patriarchy must, I think, be recognized in the customs of many groups."[40] He saw this as the survival of an original matriarchy, a theory current in Garnett's day as the result of the work of Lewis Henry Morgan, J. J. Bachofen, and other influential nineteenth-century anthropologists. It may be more accurate now, in light of heterarchical models, to say that neither patriarchy nor matriarchy is an appropriate term for designating many traditional societies, ancient Israel included.

Taken all together, these points make it seem certain that ritual behaviors surrounding the reproductive process provided Israelite women with the opportunity to experience the dignity and value, status and influence, of carrying out religious behaviors essential for the viability of their families and community. Women may have been occasional participants in extra-household community cultic events, at local shrines or even at the Jerusalem temple. But in their daily existence, they were officiants and practitioners of household praxis. Women's lives in ancient Israel were replete with opportunities for religious expression and experience.

Abbreviations

ABD	*Anchor Bible Dictionary*, 6 vols., edited by David Noel Freedman, New York: Doubleday
BAR	British Archaeological Reports
BARev	*Biblical Archaeology Review*
BASOR	*Bulletin of the American Schools of Oriental Research*
BR	*Bible Review*
CBQ	*Catholic Biblical Quarterly*
DDD	*Dictionary of Deities and Demons in the Bible*, 2d ed., edited by Karel van der Toorn, Bob Becking, and Pieter W. van der Horst, Leiden: Brill, 1999
JAAR	*Journal of the American Academy of Religion*
JBL	*Journal of Biblical Literature*
JFSR	*Journal of Feminist Studies in Religion*
JSOT	*Journal for the Study of the Old Testament*
JSOTSup	Journal for the Study of the Old Testament Supplement Series
LAI	Library of Ancient Israel
NRSV	New Revised Standard Version
OEANE	*Oxford Encyclopedia of Archaeology in the Near East*, 5 vols., edited by Eric M. Meyers et al., New York: Oxford Univ. Press, 1997

OTL   Old Testament Library
TDOT   *Theological Dictionary of the Old Testament*,
         14 vols. to date, edited by G. Johannes
         Botterweck, Helmer Ringgren, and Heinz-Josef
         Fabry, translated by John T. Willis and Geoffrey
         W. Bromiley, Grand Rapids: Eerdmans, 1977–
VTSup   Vetus Testamentum Supplements
WIS   *Women in Scripture: A Dictionary of Named*
         and Unnamed Women in the Hebrew Bible, the
         Apocryphal/Deuterocanonical Books, and
         the New Testament, edited by Carol Meyers,
         Toni Craven, and Ross S. Kraemer, Boston:
         Houghton Mifflin, 2000 (and Grand Rapids:
         Eerdmans, 2001)
ZDPV   *Zeitschrift des deutschen Palästina-Vereins*

Notes

PREFACE

1 *Congress Volume: Basel 2001*, edited by André Lemaire, VTSup 92 (Leiden: Brill, 2002).

CHAPTER 1

1 Garnett 1890–91.
2 Attributed to the Rev. Mr. Tozer in ibid., p. lxxvii.
3 Summarized by Bird 1987: 397–98. See also Wacker 1998: 17–29. A detailed discussion of several figures can be found in Selvidge 1996.
4 Peritz 1898: 114.
5 Stanton 1895–98.
6 Wellhausen 1897: 94.
7 Fohrer 1972.
8 Published in Hebrew between 1937 and 1956. The English edition (Greenberg 1960) is one volume.
9 This was really a second wave of feminist interest. The "first wave" accompanied the suffrage movement in the United States in the late-eighteenth, nineteenth, and early-twentieth centuries, represented as noted above by

the publication of *The Woman's Bible* (Stanton 1895–98). These two waves are discussed in Milne 1992.

10 As exemplified by the contributions to Brenner and Fontaine 1997. The variety of approaches is summarized in Bellis 2000a.

11 See Sered 1992: 6–8.

12 For some remarkable exceptions, see Lerner 1993.

13 So Franzmann 2000: 69–72.

14 An exception to this approach is Zevit 2001.

15 See ibid., 556.

16 For the latter, see Meyers 2000b.

17 Pointed out by Sered (1992: 7).

18 Meyers 1988: 11–13.

19 Meyers 2000d.

20 Bird 1987: 399.

21 Miller 2000: 29–45, 201–2.

22 See Meyers 2000a; Bird 1987: 403, 408–9, 422; and van der Toorn 1996: 359.

23 L. R. Klein 2000: 90–91; Meyers 1994. See also Gursky 2000.

24 See Meyers 2000c.

25 Zevit (2001: 559–62 n. 10) indicates that what appear to be four separate ritual acts are in fact, because of the structure of the chapter, a complex of rituals on a single occasion at the house of Yahweh. Cf. Darr 2000.

26 Gruber 1992: 49–68; Meyers 2000f.

27 Meyers 2000g and Eskenazi 2000; see also Eskenazi 1992.

28 See the typology in Zevit 2001: 123–24 n. 10.

CHAPTER 2

1 Zevit asserts that "Israelite religions" is a "more historically defensible term" (2001: 15 n. 10). See also his cogent

discussion of religion in chapter 1: "Surveying Paths: An Essay about Humanities, Religion, History, and Israelite Religion."

2 This understanding of religious culture is based on Cavanagh 1978 and its elaboration by Zevit (2001: 14–16 n. 10), who points out that, unlike many other definitions, this one appears to be inclusive of any system and avoids the compartmentalization of religion as a phenomenon that can be understood as either sociological or psychological.

3 Gross 1996: 81; cf. the studies collected in Falk and Gross 1989b.

4 See Orsi 1997.

5 Interestingly, contemporary feminist religionists often focus on women's biological functions as a way of understanding, reclaiming, and celebrating uniquely female processes, images, and self-identity; see King 1989: 80 and also Clark 1996 and Levine 1991.

6 Falk and Gross 1989a.

7 Meyers 1988: 112–13.

8 LeVine and LeVine 1985: 30.

9 See Burnette-Bletsch 2000a and 2000b.

10 Recognized by Bird 1987: 401 and van der Toorn 1994 and 1996.

CHAPTER 3

1 E.g., Frazer 1890; Malinowski 1955; Tylor 1924; Weber 1963.

2 Malinowski 1955: 89.

3 Fohrer 1972: 155.

4 Greenberg 1960: 79.

5 Eichrodt 1970: 173. An exception to these negative appraisals is van der Toorn 1994: 15–16.

6 A perceptive and thorough account of the association of magic with femininity, especially in east Mediterranean culture and ancient Judaism, is found in Aubin 1998: 18–52.

7 See Avalos 1995.

8 The concept of ethnohistory emerged in Europe in the 1930s and is especially prominent in American anthropology; see Fenton 1966: 75.

9 What "Israelite" means is, of course, a contested issue. Zevit (2001: 84–121) presents the evidence that a self-identified people, an ethnic group known as Israelites, occupied at least parts of the highlands of Canaan from the twelfth century BCE on.

10 Rapoport 1994: 461.

11 Wilk and Rathje 1982: 618.

12 See Stager 1985; McNutt 1999: 152, 168.

13 Meyers 1991.

14 See Zevit 2001: 123–24 for definitions of types and chart 1 (p. 248) for a summary of the data.

15 See Dozeman 2004: 34–35.

16 E.g., Bird 1989; van der Toorn 1994 and 1996; Albertz 1994: 39; Miller 2000: 62–76.

17 Bird 1989: 296. She does, however, wonder if there are other undocumented rituals that women controlled (292, 297).

18 Albertz 1994: 39. This is in reference to "patriarchal" or pre-state religion, which he assumes (187) to have continued during the monarchy.

CHAPTER 4

1 For a discussion of terminology and typology, see Kletter 1996: 28–30.

2 See Kletter 1996: 10–27 for a history of research. Other major studies include those of Pilz 1924; Pritchard 1943; Holland 1975 and 1977; Engle 1979; Keel and Uehlinger 1998; and Winter 1983. See also Hadley 2000.

3 Kletter summarizes the various goddess theories (1996: 74–77).

4 For a summary of the attributes of figurines in relation to their functions, see Voigt 2000, especially table 2 (261–62).

5 Ibid., 258.

6 See Meyers 1988: 162–63. Van der Toorn also supports the notion that figures that are pregnant, nursing, or holding a child depict human females (1994: 91). Note that Pritchard, despairing of identifying the terra-cottas with goddesses, astutely suggests that the pillar-figurine functioned as a "talisman associated with childbearing" (1943: 87).

7 Frymer-Kensky calls them a "visual metaphor" (1992: 159).

8 See Kletter 1996: 45–46, 141, and appendices 1, 2, 4, 5.

9 Ibid., 58–62.

10 Stager 1985: 15–16; Holladay 1997: 339–40; and Herr and Clark 2001: 45, 47.

11 Bloch-Smith 1992: 148, 150.

12 The statistics provided by Holladay (1987: 276) for four sites (Beer-sheba, Tell Beit Mirsim, Tell en-Nasbeh, and Hazor) suggest an average of one per household. Daviau's findings (2001: 202–3) suggest an even higher number per household. Moreover, if a household consisted of several domestic components serving an extended family, the number of figurines in a household might be even more numerous.

13 Meshel 1992; see especially the drawing on p. 1462.

14 The corpus of such artifacts is summarized in Keel and Uehlinger 1998: 217–23, 259–60. Late Bronze Age

precursors, all from the end of that period and similar to objects from Amarna, are collected in McGovern 1985: 16–17.

15 Dever 1984: 25. See also Wilson 1976.

16 E.g., at Gezer, so Keel and Uehlinger 1998: 220 and illustration 225e.

17 Zevit 2001: 606, 649.

18 Pinch 1994: 44. The unusual frontal stance of Bes figures in Egyptian art suggests to some an origin outside of Egypt, perhaps in Mesopotamia. See also Robins 1993: 85 and te Velde 1999: 173.

19 For example, the Lachish examples are from both tombs and domestic structures; Murray 1953: 378–79, plates 34:7, 12–14; 35:45, 46; 36:48. Dever connects Bes amulets in tombs with what he calls "Astarte" figurines (1984: 26), by which he probably means pillar-figurines (as Keel and Uehlinger suggest [1998: 240 n. 114]).

20 Fleming 1955.

21 So Keel and Uehlinger 1998: 333; van der Toorn 1994: 91.

22 Beit-Arieh 1973: 35–6 and plates 27:1–3, 71:1–3.

23 Zevit 2001: 175–76.

CHAPTER 5

1 The formality of a vow (see Cartledge 1992: 185–93) may be the reason that it is not made in the household; such women's vows at a shrine may have been one way—a very serious step—for women to deal with childlessness.

2 The evidence for fertility prayers and/or rituals taking place in households as well as shrines is reviewed by Gursky (2000: 17–31), who points out that Ugaritic texts depict similar locations for prayers for an heir.

3 Stol (2000: 52–59) describes these and other texts in detail.

4 Avalos 1997: 454; Stol 2000: 56–58.

5 See Gursky 2000: 58–72.

6 Cited in ibid., 60 n. 6. See also Stol 2000: 49 for colored wool as part of an amulet.

7 Driver 1950: 63–65.

8 Eising 1997: 332.

9 A better translation than NRSV's "capable wife"; cf. Fontaine 1998: 160.

10 See Meyers 1999c: 119–21.

11 Bohmbach 2000: 38. Perhaps a glimpse of this appropriation by the biblical redactor of a mother's role to the father is visible in the fact that the naming of Solomon is done by Bathsheba according to *qĕrê* and by David according to *kĕtîb*.

12 See the discussion in Gursky 2000: 94–134 and in Neff 1969: 55, 81, 151.

13 De Vaux 1961: 43. Thus, to efface a name meant to destroy the person (e.g., Deut 7:24; 9:14; 12:3).

14 So understood by Bird 1989: 297; Propp 1998: 236; and Pardes 1992: 78–97.

15 The latter is a suggestion of Bellis (2000b).

16 Pinch 1994.

17 Barns 1956: 26, plate 17:1.15.

18 Robins 1993: 82–87.

19 Pinch 1994: 115. The "evil eye," or *wedjat*, images found in Syro-Palestinian assemblages would be part of this grouping. See Willet 1999: 330–76 for a discussion of the evil eye as it appears in artifacts, in texts from the Bible, and in the ethnographic record. For the presence of the "evil eye" in the Hebrew Bible and the biblical world, see Elliott 1991: 147–59, 332–36.

20 Cited in Robins 1993: 86.

21 Scurlock 1991. For examples, see Foster 1995: 393–99. See also the detailed discussion of pregnancy problems, the

use of magic, childbirth and childcare procedures and professionals, and related topics in Stol 2000.

22 See Fontaine 2000; Hutter 1999; Foster 1995: 400–405; and Wiggermann 2000.

23 Summarized by Willett 1999: 178–96; cf. van der Toorn 1996: 25 and Stol 2000: 49–52, 116, 132–33, 166. The use of amulets was probably accompanied by the chanting of incantations.

24 Nougayrol 1969.

25 Beckman 1983.

26 Babylonian Talmud, *Shabbat* 129b.

27 Naveh and Shaked 1993: 101–5, 142–45.

28 A discussion of *lamellae* is found in Aubin 1998: 203–17.

29 M. Klein 2000: 38.

CHAPTER 6

1 Carter (1997) summarizes the pitfalls and advantages of using ethnographic materials.

2 A compendious collection of such materials in Jewish tradition, from antiquity to the present and from a wide variety of Sephardic and Ashkenazic Jewish communities, is found in M. Klein 2000. Christian, Jewish, and Arab traditions in the Mediterranean world are recorded in travelers' accounts (such as Garnett 1890–91) and ethnographies (such as Morgenstern 1966 and Granqvist 1947).

3 See Willett 1999: 330–47 for specific examples. See also Morgenstern 1966: 21; M. Klein 2000: 180–81; cf. Sered 1992: 56–58.

4 Garnett 1890–91, (vol 2): 68.

5 Described in Sered 1992: 20–21.

6 M. Klein 2000: 184–85.

7 Te Velde 1999.

8 Garnett 1890–91 (vol 2): 472–73.

9 Ibid., (vol 2): 245.

10 See Morgenstern 1966: 7–8, 13, 15; Garnett 1890–91 (vol 1): 69, 315; Granqvist 1947: 74, 98–101, 242–43; M. Klein 2000: 191, 193.

11 Described in Sered 1992: 18–29. Bird draws heavily on Sered in suggesting a vital role for women in ancestor cults (1991: 98–102).

12 Related to me by a senior member of the Jewish community in Durham, North Carolina.

13 See http://israelvisit.co.il/Rachel/.

CHAPTER 7

1 See Beckman 1983: 34; Stol 2000: 11–12, 59–70, 129–31; and M. Klein 2000: 125, 142–46, 149–51.

2 As by Gottwald (1979: 237–92) and Wright (1992: 761–62).

3 Sharer and Ashmore 1987: 439.

4 Faust 2000; McNutt 1999: 152, 168; cf. Frick 1997 and Fritz 1997.

5 Lenski 1984: 198–200. Similar percentages have been calculated for many other regions of the world.

6 These terms and other designations for settlements are discussed in B. A. Levine 1999. Because most "cities" mentioned in the Hebrew Bible were not truly urban centers, and because the spatial practices with respect to gender in nineteenth-century and later Middle Eastern cities cannot be used as meaningful analogues to those of Iron Age Syro-Palestinian settlements, the theory of de Geus about Iron Age cities and their residents seems flawed (1997: 75–86).

7 Hopkins 1985: 213–34.

8 Meyers 1999a: 154–58.

9 Sered 1996: 21.

10 Even the well-meaning work of Gerstenberger calls men's religious structures "higher" (1996: 55).
11 So Albertz (1994: 39), who also claims that cultic practices for dealing with sickness or disease meant summoning *male* cultic personnel (101).
12 Peoples and Bailey 1988: 320.
13 See Meyers 2000e; cf. Towler and Bramall 1986.
14 Hackett 2000.
15 Gruber 2000.
16 See Overholt 2000.
17 Bloch-Smith 1992: 100.
18 So van der Toorn 1990: 203–22; cf. Lewis 1999: 849 and Bird 1989: 296 n. 36.
19 Arnold 2004.
20 Brenner 1997: 84–86. Such an explanation is more tenable than van der Toorn's claim that women used witchcraft and sorcery to take revenge for their subordination (1994: 116).
21 So Avalos 1995: 295–97.
22 Bowen 1999.
23 See the discussion in Meyers 1999a: 161–62. This understanding of guilds is based on the observations of Mendelsohn (1940: 17–21).
24 See Avalos 1997: 45 and Stol 2000: 171–76.
25 Described in Meyers 2003.
26 Meyers 1999c: 122–27. Perhaps they helped form what Gottwald calls a "protective association of families" (1979: 257–67).
27 Taylor 2002.
28 Franzmann 2000: 79–81.
29 As Albertz 1994: 194.
30 Bechtel 1994: 21–22.
31 See Nelson 1999: 186–87.
32 Meyers 1999b.

33 Meyers 2003.
34 Gross 1996: 23. Cf. the discussion of patriarchy as a problematic category in Meyers 1988: 24–46. See also Young 1999: 176.
35 Nelson 1999: 184–85.
36 The anthropology of gender shows that gender complementarity, with same-sex groups providing discrete contributions to household and community life, is more typical than gender hierarchy in many instances; see Gilchrist 1999: 8, 48–50, 52, 98.
37 Levy 1999: 71–74.
38 Explained in Meyers 2006.
39 Crumley 1979: 144.
40 Stuart-Glennie 1891: 572–73, 597.

Bibliography

Albertz, Rainer. 1994. *A History of Israelite Religion in the Old Testament Period. Volume 1: From the Beginning to the End of the Monarchy.* Translated by John Bowden. OTL. Louisville: Westminster John Knox.

Arnold, Bill T. 2004. "Necromancy and Cleromancy in 1 and 2 Samuel." *CBQ* 66:199–213.

Aubin, Melissa A. 1998. "Gendering Magic in Late Antique Judaism." Ph.D. dissertation, Duke Univ.

Avalos, Hector I. 1995. *Illness and Health Care in the Ancient Near East: The Role of the Temple in Greece, Mesopotamia, and Israel.* Harvard Semitic Monographs 54. Atlanta: Scholars.

———. 1997. "Medicine." In *OEANE* 3:450–59.

Barns, John W. B., editor. 1956. *Five Ramesseum Papyri.* Oxford: Griffiths Institute at the Univ. Press.

Bechtel, Lyn M. 1994. "What If Dinah Is Not Raped? (Genesis 34)." *JSOT* 62:19–36.

Beckman, Gary M. 1983. *Hittite Birth Rituals.* Studien zu den Boğazköy-Texten 29. Wiesbaden: Harrassowitz.

Beit-Arieh, Izhaq. 1973. "The Western Quarter." In *Beersheba I, Excavations at Tel Beersheba, 1969–71 Seasons*, edited by Yohanan Aharoni. Tel Aviv: Tel Aviv Univ. Institute of Archaeology.

Bellis, Alice O. 2000a. "Feminist Biblical Scholarship." In *WIS*, 24–32.

———. 2000b. "Zipporah: Issues of Race, Religion, Gender and Power." Lecture at Duke Univ., Durham, North Carolina.

Bird, Phyllis. 1987. "The Place of Women in the Israelite Cultus." In Miller, Hanson, and McBride 1987, 397–419.

———. 1989. "Women's Religion in Ancient Israel." In *Women's Earliest Records: From Ancient Egypt and Western Asia*, edited by Barbara S. Lesko, 283–98. Brown Judaic Studies 166. Atlanta: Scholars.

———. 1991. "Israelite Religion and the Faith of Israel's Daughters." In *The Bible and the Politics of Exegesis: Essays in Honor of Norman K. Gottwald on His Sixty-fifth Birthday*, edited by David Jobling, Peggy L. Day, and Gerald T. Sheppard, 97–108. Cleveland: Pilgrim.

Bloch-Smith, Elizabeth. 1992. *Judahite Burial Practices and Beliefs about the Dead*. JSOTSup 123. Sheffield: Sheffield Academic.

Bohmbach, Karla G. 2000. "Names and Naming in the Biblical World." In *WIS*, 33–39.

Bowen, Nancy. 1999. "The Daughters of Your People: Female Prophets in Ezekiel 13:17–23." *JBL* 118:417–33.

Brenner, Athalya. 1997. *The Intercourse of Knowledge: On Gendering Desire and 'Sexuality' in the Hebrew Bible*. Biblical Interpretation Series 26. Leiden: Brill.

Brenner, Athalya, and Carole Fontaine, editors. 1997. *A Feminist Companion to Reading the Bible: Approaches, Methods and Strategies*. Feminist Companion to the Bible. Sheffield: Sheffield Academic.

Burnette-Bletsch, Rhonda. 2000a. "Women after Childbirth (Lev 12:1–8)." In *WIS*, 204.

———. 2000b. "Women and Bodily Emissions (Lev 15:18–33; 18:19; 20:18)." In *WIS*, 205–6.

Carter, Charles E. 1997. "Ethnoarchaeology." In *OEANE* 2:280–84.

Cartledge, Tony W. 1992. *Vows in the Hebrew Bible and the Ancient Near East*. JSOTSup 147. Sheffield: JSOT Press.

Cavanagh, Ronald R. 1978. "The Term Religion." In *Introduction to the Study of Religion*, edited by T. William Hall, 1–19. New York: Harper & Row.

Clark, Linda S. 1996. "Rituals, Women's." In *Dictionary of Feminist Theologies*, edited by Letty M. Russell and J. Shannon Clark, 251. Louisville: Westminster John Knox.

Crumley, Carole L. 1979. "Three Locational Models: An Epistemological Assessment of Anthropology and Archaeology." In *Advances in Archaeological Method*, edited by Michael B. Schiffer, 2:141–73. New York: Academic.

Darr, Katheryn Pfisterer. 2000. "Women Weeping for Tammuz (Ezek 8:14)." In *WIS*, 335–36.

Daviau, P. M. Michèle. 2001. "Family Religion: Evidence for the Paraphernalia of the Domestic Cult." In *The World of the Arameans II: Studies in History and Archaeology in Honor of Paul-Eugène Dion*, edited by P. M. Michèle Daviau, John W. Wevers, and Michael Weigl, 199–229. JSOTSup 325. Sheffield: Sheffield Academic.

de Geus, C. H. J. 1997. "The City of Women: Women's Places in Ancient Israelite Cities." In *Congress Volume: Cambridge 1995*, edited by John A. Emerton, 75–86. VTSup 66. Leiden: Brill.

de Vaux, Roland. 1961. *Ancient Israel: Its Life and Institutions*. Translated by John McHugh. New York: McGraw-Hill.

Dever, William G. 1984. "Asherah, Consort of Yahweh? New Evidence from Kuntillet ʿAjrûd." *BASOR* 255:21–37.

Dozeman, Thomas B. 2004. "The Holiness of God in Contemporary Jewish and Christian Theology." In *God's Word for Our World: Theological and Cultural Studies in Honor of Simon John De Vries*, edited by J. Harold Ellens, Deborah L. Ellens, Rolf P. Knierim, and Isaac Kalimi, 1:24–36. JSOTSup 389. New York: T & T Clark International.

Driver, Samuel R. 1950. "Difficult Words in the Hebrew Prophets." In *Studies in Old Testament Prophecy, Presented to Theodore H. Robinson on His Sixty-fifth Birthday*, edited by H. H. Rowley, 52–72. Edinburgh: T & T Clark.

Eichrodt, Walther. 1970. *Ezekiel*. Translated by Cosslett Quin. OTL. Philadelphia: Westminster.

Eising, Hermann. 1997. "*melaḥ*." In *TDOT* 7:331–33.

Elliott, John H. 1991. "The Evil Eye in the First Testament: The Ecology and Culture of a Pervasive Belief." In *The Bible and the Politics of Exegesis: Essays in Honor of Norman K. Gottwald on His Sixty-fifth Birthday*, edited by David Jobling, Peggy L. Day, and Gerald T. Sheppard, 147–59, 332–36. Cleveland: Pilgrim.

Engle, James R. 1979. "Pillar Figurines of Iron Age Israel and Asherah/Asherim." Ph.D. dissertation, Univ. of Pittsburgh.

Eskenazi, Tamara C. 1992. "Out from the Shadow: Biblical Women in the Postexilic Era." *JSOT* 54:225–43.

———. 2000. "Women, Part of the Assembly of the People (Neh 8:2; 10:28; 12:43)." In *WIS*, 288.

Falk, Nancy A., and Rita M. Gross. 1989a. "In the Wings: Rituals for Wives and Mothers." In *Unspoken Words: Women's Religious Lives*, edited by Nancy A. Falk and Rita M. Gross, 57–58. Belmont, Calif.: Wadsworth.

———, editors. 1989b. *Unspoken Words: Women's Religious Lives*. Belmont, Calif.: Wadsworth.

Faust, Avraham. 2000. "The Rural Community in Ancient Israel during the Iron Age II." *BASOR* 317:17–39.

Fenton, William N. 1966. "Fieldwork, Museum Studies, and Ethnohistory." *Ethnohistory* 13:71–85.

Fleming, Daniel J. 1955. "Religious Symbols Crossing Cultural Boundaries." In *Religious Symbolism*, edited by F. Ernest Johnson, 81–106. Port Washington, N.Y.: Institute for Religious and Social Studies.

Fohrer, Georg. 1972. *History of Israelite Religion*. Translated by David E. Green. Nashville: Abingdon. German ed. 1968.

Fontaine, Carole R. 1998. "Proverbs." In *Women's Bible Commentary*, edited by Carole A. Newsom and Sharon H. Ringe, 153–60. Louisville: Westminster John Knox.

———. 2000. "Lilith." In *WIS*, 531.

Foster, Benjamin R. 1995. *From Distant Days: Myths, Tales, and Poetry of Ancient Mesopotamia*. Bethesda, Md.: CDL Press.

Franzmann, Majella. 2000. *Women and Religion*. New York: Oxford Univ. Press.

Frazer, James G. 1890. *The Golden Bough: Part 1, The Magic Art and the Evolution of Kings*. London: Macmillan.

Frick, Frank S. 1997. "Cities: An Overview." In *OEANE* 2:14–19.

Fritz, Volkmar. 1997. "Cities of the Bronze and Iron Ages." In *OEANE* 2:19–24.

Frymer-Kensky, Tikva. 1992. *In the Wake of the Goddesses: Women, Culture, and the Biblical Transformation of Pagan Myth*. New York: Free Press.

Garnett, Lucy M. S. 1890–91. *The Women of Turkey and Their Folklore*. 2 vols. London: David Nutt.

Gerstenberger, Erhard S. 1996. *Yahweh the Patriarch: Ancient Images of God and Feminist Theology*. Translated by Frederick J. Gaiser. Minneapolis: Fortress Press.

Gilchrist, Roberta. 1999. *Gender and Archaeology: Contesting the Past*. London: Routledge.

Gottwald, Norman K. 1979. *The Tribes of Yahweh: A Sociology of the Religion of Liberated Israel, 1250–1050 BCE*. Maryknoll, N.Y.: Orbis.

Granqvist, Hilma Natalia. 1947. *Birth and Childhood among the Arabs: Studies in a Muhammadan Village in Palestine*. Helsingfors: Söderström.

Greenberg, Moshe. 1960. *The Religion of Israel*. Chicago: Univ. of Chicago Press. Translation and abridgment of Kaufmann 1937–56.

Gross, Rita. 1996. *Feminism and Religion: An Introduction*. Boston: Beacon.

Gruber, Mayer I. 1992. "Women in the Cult according to the Priestly Code." In *The Motherhood of God and Other Studies*, 49–69. South Florida Studies in the History of Judaism 57. Atlanta: Scholars.

———. 2000. "Puah." In *WIS*, 137–38.

Gursky, Marjorie D. 2000. "Reproductive Rituals in Biblical Israel." Ph.D. dissertation, New York Univ.

Hackett, Jo Ann. 2000. "Women Attending the Wife of Phinehas (1 Sam 4:20)." In *WIS*, 255.

Hadley, Judith M. 2000. *The Cult of Asherah in Ancient Israel and Judah: Evidence for a Hebrew Goddess*. Univ. of Cambridge Oriental Publications 57. Cambridge: Cambridge Univ. Press.

Herr, Larry G., and Douglas R. Clark. 2001. "Excavating the Tribe of Reuben." *BARev* 27:36–47, 64, 66.

Holladay, John S., Jr. 1987. "Religion in Israel and Judah under the Monarchy: An Explicitly Archaeological Approach." In Miller, Hanson, and McBride 1987:249–99.

———. 1997. "Four-Room House." In *OEANE* 2:337–42.

Holland, Thomas A. 1975. "A Typological and Archaeological Study of Human and Animal Representation in the Plastic Art of Palestine." Ph.D. dissertation, Oxford Univ.

———. 1977. "A Study of Palestinian Iron Age Baked Clay Figurines with Special Reference to Jerusalem Cave 1." *Levant* 9:121–55.

Hopkins, David C. 1985. *The Highlands of Canaan: Agricultural Life in the Early Iron Age*. Social World of Biblical Antiquity Series 3. Sheffield: Almond.

Hutter, M. 1999. "Lilith." In *DDD*, 520–21.

Kaufmann, Yehezkel. 1937–56. *Toledot Ha'emunah HaYisraelit Me-yamai Kedem ad Sof Bet Sheni*. 8 vols. Tel Aviv: Musad Bialik.

Keel, Othmar, and Christoph Uehlinger. 1998. *Gods, Goddesses, and Images of God in Ancient Israel*. Translated by Thomas H. Trapp. Minneapolis: Fortress. German ed. 1992.

King, Ursula. 1989. *Women and Spirituality: Voices of Protest and Promise*. London: Croom Helm.

Klein, Lillian R. 2000. "Hannah." In *WIS*, 90–91.

Klein, Michele. 2000. *A Time to Be Born: Customs and Folklore of Jewish Birth*. Philadelphia: Jewish Publication Society.

Kletter, Raz. 1996. *The Archaeology of the Judean Pillar-Figurines and the Archaeology of Asherah*. BAR International Series 636. Oxford: Tempus Reparatum.

Lenski, Gerhard E. 1984. *Power and Privilege: A Theory of Social Stratification*. 3d ed. Chapel Hill: Univ. of North Carolina Press.

Lerner, Gerda. 1993. *The Creation of Feminist Consciousness: From the Middle Ages to 1870 A.D.* Women and History 2. New York: Oxford Univ. Press.

Levine, Baruch A. 1999. "The Biblical Town as Reality and Typology: Evaluating Biblical References to Towns and Their Functions." In *Urbanization and Land Ownership in the Ancient Near East*, edited by Michael Hudson and Baruch A. Levine, 2:421–53. Cambridge:

Peabody Museum of Archaeology and Ethnology, Harvard Univ.

Levine, Elizabeth R. 1991. *A Ceremonies Sampler: New Rites, Celebrations, and Observances of Jewish Women*. San Diego: Women's Institute for Continuing Jewish Education.

LeVine, Sarah, and Robert A. LeVine. 1985. "Life Courses in Agrarian Societies." In *Gender and the Life Course*, edited by Alice S. Rossi, 29–42. New York: Aldine.

Levy, Janet. 1999. "Gender, Power, and Heterarchy in Middle-Level Societies." In *Manifesting Power: Gender and the Interpretation of Power in Archaeology*, edited by Tracy L. Sweely, 62–78. London: Routledge.

Lewis, Theodore J. 1999. "Teraphim." In *DDD*, 844–50.

Malinowski, Bronislaw. 1955. *Magic, Science and Religion, and Other Essays*. Garden City, N.Y.: Doubleday. (Orig. pub. 1925.)

McGovern, Patrick E. 1985. *Late Bronze Palestinian Pendants: Innovation in a Cosmopolitan Age*. Sheffield: JSOT Press.

McNutt, Paula. 1999. *Reconstructing the Society of Ancient Israel*. LAI. Louisville: Westminster John Knox.

Mendelsohn, Isaac. 1940. "Guilds in Ancient Palestine." *BASOR* 80:17–21.

Meshel, Zeev. 1992. "Teman, Ḥorvat." In *The New Encyclopedia of Archaeological Excavations in the Holy Land*, edited by Ephraim Stern, 4:1458–64. Jerusalem: Israel Exploration Society and Carta.

Meyers, Carol. 1988. *Discovering Eve: Ancient Israelite Women in Context*. New York: Oxford Univ. Press.

———. 1991. "'To Her Mother's House'—Considering a Counterpart to the Israelite *Bêt 'āb*." In *The Bible and the Politics of Exegesis: Essays in Honor of Norman K. Gottwald on His Sixty-fifth Birthday*, edited by David

Jobling, Peggy Day, and Gerald Sheppard, 39–51, 304–7. New York: Pilgrim.

———. 1994. "Hannah and Her Sacrifice: Reclaiming Female Agency." In *A Feminist Companion to Samuel and Kings*, edited by Athalya Brenner, 93–104. Feminist Companion to the Bible 5. Sheffield: Sheffield Academic.

———. 1999a. "Guilds and Gatherings: Women's Groups in Ancient Israel." In *Realia Dei: Essays in Archaeology and Biblical Interpretation in Honor of Edward F. Campbell, Jr. at His Retirement*, edited by Prescott H. Williams Jr. and Theodore Hiebert, 154–84. Scholars Press Homage Series 23. Atlanta: Scholars.

———. 1999b. "Mother to Muse: An Archaeomusicological Study of Women's Performance in Ancient Israel." In *Recycling Biblical Figures. Papers Read at a NOSTER Colloquium in Amsterdam, 12–13 May 1997*, edited by Athalya Brenner and Jan Willem van Henten, 50–77. Leiden: Deo.

———. 1999c. "'Women in the Neighborhood' (Ruth 4.17)'—Informal Female Networks in Ancient Israel." In *Ruth and Esther*, edited by Athalya Brenner, 110–27. Feminist Companion to the Bible 2/3. Sheffield: Sheffield Academic.

———. 2000a. "Daughters (and Sons) and Female (and Male) Slaves Rejoicing (Deut 12:12; 16:11, 14)." In *WIS*, 224.

———. 2000b. "Female Images of God in the Hebrew Bible." In *WIS*, 525–28.

———. 2000c. "Israelite Women in the Covenant Community (Deut 29:11; 31:12; Josh 8:35)." In *WIS*, 235–36.

———. 2000d. "Medium/Wizard (Lev 20:27)." In *WIS*, 212.

———. 2000e. "Midwife (Gen 35:17; 38:28)." In *WIS*, 182–83.

———. 2000f. "Person (Male or Female) Presenting an Offering (Lev 2:1; also Lev 4:2, 27; 5:1–2, 4, 15, 17, 21, 25, 27; 23:29–30B; Num 5:6; 15:27, 30; 19:22; 31:19, 28; 35:11, 15, 30B)." In *WIS*, 203.

———. 2000g. "Women (and Men and Children) in Assembly (Ezra 10:1)." In *WIS*, 286.

———. 2003. "Material Remains and Social Relations: Women's Culture in Agrarian Households of the Iron Age." In *Symbiosis, Symbolism, and the Power of the Past: Canaan, Ancient Israel, and Their Neighbors from the Late Bronze Age through Roman Palestine*, edited by William G. Dever and Seymour Gitin, 425–44. Winona Lake, Ind.: Eisenbrauns.

———. 2006. "Hierarchy or Heterarchy? Archaeology and the Theorizing of Israelite Society." In *Confronting the Past: Essays in Honor of William G. Dever*, edited by Seymour Gitin, J. Edward Wright, and J. P. Dessel, 245–54. Winona Lake, Ind.: Eisenbrauns.

Miller, Patrick D. 2000. *The Religion of Ancient Israel*. LAI. Louisville: Westminster John Knox.

Miller, Patrick D., Jr., Paul D. Hanson, and S. Dean McBride, editors. 1987. *Ancient Israelite Religion: Essays in Honor of Frank Moore Cross*. Philadelphia: Fortress Press.

Milne, Pamela M. 1992. "Feminist Interpretations of the Bible: Then and Now." *BR* 8:38–43, 52–55.

Morgenstern, Julian. 1966. *Rites of Birth, Marriage, Death and Kindred Occasions among the Semites*. Cincinnati: Hebrew Union College Press.

Murray, Margaret A. 1953. "The Faience Objects." In Olga Tufnell et al., *Lachish III: The Iron Age*, 378–81. London: Oxford Univ. Press.

Naveh, Joseph, and Shaul Shaked. 1993. *Magic Spells and Formulae: Aramaic Incantations of Late Antiquity*. Jerusalem: Magnes.

Neff, Robert W. 1969. "Announcement in Old Testament Birth Stories." Ph.D. dissertation, Yale Univ.

Nelson, Sarah M. 1999. "Rethinking Gender and Power." In *Manifesting Power: Gender and the Interpretation of*

Power in Archaeology, edited by Tracy L. Sweely, 184–89. London: Routledge.

Nougayrol, Jean. 1969. "La Lameštu à Ugarit." In *Ugaritica VI*. Mission de Ras Shamra 17. Paris: Geuthner.

Orsi, Robert. 1997. "Everyday Miracles: The Study of Lived Religion." In *Lived Religion in America: Toward a History of Practice*, edited by David D. Hall, 3–21. Princeton, N.J.: Princeton Univ. Press.

Overholt, Thomas W. 2000. "The Medium of Endor (1 Sam 28:7–25)." In *WIS*, 258–59.

Pardes, Ilana. 1992. *Countertraditions in the Bible: A Feminist Approach*. Cambridge: Harvard Univ. Press.

Peoples, James, and Garrick Bailey. 1988. *Humanity: An Introduction to Cultural Anthropology*. St. Paul: West.

Peritz, Ismar J. 1898. "Women in the Ancient Hebrew Cult." *JBL* 17:111–48.

Pilz, Edwin. 1924. "Die weiblischen Gottheiten Kanaans." *ZDPV* 47:129–68.

Pinch, Geraldine. 1995. *Magic in Ancient Egypt*. Austin: Univ. of Texas Press.

Pritchard, James B. 1943. *Palestinian Figurines in Relation to Certain Goddesses Known through Literature*. American Oriental Series 24. New Haven, Conn.: American Oriental Society.

Propp, William H. C. 1998. *Exodus 1–18*. Anchor Bible 2. New York: Doubleday.

Rapoport, Amos. 1994. "Spatial Organization and the Built Environment." In *Companion Encyclopedia of Anthropology*, edited by Tim Ingold, 460–502. London: Routledge.

Robins, Gay. 1993. *Women in Ancient Egypt*. Cambridge: Harvard Univ. Press.

Scurlock, JoAnne. 1991. "Baby-snatching Demons, Restless Souls, and the Dangers of Childbirth: Magico-medical

Means of Dealing with Some of the Perils of Motherhood in Ancient Mesopotamia." *Incognita* 2:135–83.

Selvidge, Marla J. 1996. *Notorious Voices: Feminist Biblical Interpretation 1550–1920*. New York: Continuum.

Sered, Susan Starr. 1992. *Women as Ritual Experts: The Religious Lives of Elderly Jewish Women in Jerusalem*. New York: Oxford Univ. Press.

———. 1996. "Mother Love, Child Death, and Religious Innovation." *JFSR* 12:5–23.

Sharer, Robert J., and Wendy Ashmore. 1987. *Archaeology: Discovering Our Past*. Palo Alto, Calif.: Mayfield.

Stager, Lawrence E. 1985. "The Archaeology of the Family in Ancient Israel." *BASOR* 260:1–35.

Stanton, Elizabeth Cady. 1895–98. *The Woman's Bible*. 2 vols. New York: Arno.

Stol, Marten. 2000. *Birth in Babylonia and the Bible: Its Mediterranean Setting*. Cuneiform Monographs 14. Groningen: Styx.

Stuart-Glennie, John S. 1891. "The Origins of Matriarchy." In Lucy M. J. Garnett, *The Women of Turkey and Their Folklore*, 2:547–616. London: David Nutt.

Taylor, Shelley E. 2002. "Women Befriending." In *The Tending Instinct: How Nurturing Is Essential for Who We Are and How We Live*, 88–113. New York: Holt.

te Velde, Herman. 1999. "Bes." In *DDD*, 173.

Towler, Jean, and Joan Bramall. 1986. *Midwives in History and Society*. London: Croom Helm.

Tylor, Edward B. 1924. *Primitive Culture*. 7th ed. New York: Brentano. (Orig. pub. 1871.)

van der Toorn, Karel. 1990. "The Nature of the Biblical Teraphim in Light of the Cuneiform Evidence." *CBQ* 52:203–22.

———. 1994. *From Her Cradle to Her Grave: The Role of Religion in the Life of the Israelite and the Babylonian Woman*.

Translated by Sarah J. Denning-Bolle. Biblical Seminar 23. Sheffield: JSOT Press.

———. 1996. *Family Religion in Babylonia, Syria, and Israel: Continuity and Change in the Forms of Religious Life.* Studies in the History and Culture of the Ancient Near East 7. Leiden: Brill.

Voigt, Mary M. 2000. "Çatal Hüyük in Context: Ritual at Early Neolithic Sites in Central and Eastern Turkey." In *Life in Neolithic Farming Communities: Social Organization, Identity, and Differentiation,* edited by Ian Kuij, 253–93. New York: Kluwer Academic/Plenum.

Wacker, Marie-Theres. 1998. "Historical, Hermeneutical, and Methodological Foundations." In *Feminist Interpretation: The Bible in Women's Perspective,* edited by Luisa Schotroff, Silvia Shroer, and Marie-Theres Wacker, translated by Marten Rumscheidt and Barbara Rumscheidt, 17–29. Minneapolis: Fortress Press.

Weber, Max. 1963. *Sociology of Religion.* Translated by Ephraim Fischoff. Boston: Beacon. German ed. 1922.

Wellhausen, Julius. 1897. *Israelitische und jüdische Geschichte.* 3d ed. Berlin: Reimer.

Wiggermann, F. A. M. 2000. "Lamaštu, Daughter of Anu, a Profile." In Marten Stol, *Birth in Babylonia and the Bible: Its Mediterranean Setting,* 217–52. Cuneiform Monographs 14. Groningen: Styx.

Wilk, Richard R., and William L. Rathje. 1982. "Household Archaeology." *American Behavioral Scientist* 25:617–39.

Willett, Elizabeth A. R. 1999. "Women and Household Shrines in Ancient Israel." Ph.D. dissertation, Univ. of Arizona.

Wilson, V. 1976. "The Iconography of Bes with Particular Reference to the Cypriot Influence." *Levant* 7:77–103.

Winter, Urs. 1983. *Frau und Göttin: Exegetische und ikonographische Studien zum weiblichen Gottesbild im Alten*

Israel und in dessen Umvelt. Orbis biblicus et orientalis 53. Göttingen: Vandenhoeck & Ruprecht.

Wright, C. J. H. 1992. "Family." In *ABD* 2:761–69.

Young, Katherine K. 1999. "Having Your Cake and Eating It Too: Feminism and Religion." *JAAR* 67:167–84.

Zevit, Ziony. 2001. *Religions of Ancient Israel: A Synthesis of Parallactic Approaches*. New York: Continuum.